Louie
STILL GOT IT, NEVER LOST IT!
MY STORY

Louie

STILL GOT IT, NEVER LOST IT!
MY STORY

Louie Spence

HARPER

HARPER

An imprint of HarperCollins*Publishers*
77–85 Fulham Palace Road,
Hammersmith, London W6 8JB

www.harpercollins.co.uk

First published by HarperCollins*Publishers* 2011

This paperback edition published 2012

1 3 5 7 9 10 8 6 4 2

Lovin' You
Words and Music by Minnie Riperton and Richard Rudolph
© Copyright 1972 (Renewed) by Embassy Music Corporation (BMI) and Dickiebird
Music (BMI).
Dickiebird Music administered Worldwide by Embassy Music Corporation (BMI)
All Rights Reserved. International Copyright Secured
Reprinted by Permission.

Your Song
Words and Music by Elton John and Bernie Taupin
© Copyright 1969 Dick James Music Limited.
Universal/Dick James Music Limited.
All rights in Germany administered by Universal Music Publ. GmbH.
All Rights Reserved. International Copyright Secured.
Used by permission of Music Sales Limited.

A catalogue record of this book
is available from the British Library

ISBN 978-0-00-744771-8

Printed and bound in Great Britain by
Clays Ltd, St Ives plc

MIX
Paper from
responsible sources
FSC FSC™ C007454

Find out more about HarperCollins and the environment at
www.harpercollins.co.uk/green

Contents

Louie Spence

Acknowledgements

There are a few people I would like to thank for something I thought would never be possible. I *say* I thought it wouldn't be possible – I never even thought about it, until someone approached me about writing this book: Natalie Jerome, from HarperCollins. Obviously, she didn't know that I didn't know where to put a comma, apostrophe, or question mark! And the only things I could spell were *Louie Spence* and *Dance*.

Then there's my fabulous agent, Vivienne Clore, affectionately known in the industry as 'The Claw', who takes no hostages and speaks no bullshit! She speaks in pound signs, which is always good by me. Although I could never spell, I always knew the price of a pint of milk. I could start my own dairy farm now, thanks to her hard work.

And finally, and most importantly, this book would definitely not exist if it wasn't for my dear friend Caleb Newman. Even before the success of the Sky1 TV show *Pineapple Dance Studios*, he said I should write. Not necessarily a book – just that I should write. He always said I was a natural storyteller – hopefully after reading this book, you will agree with him. He made me feel like Barbara Cartland as I lay on the sofa, the floor, the roof, and sat on the loo dictating my life story. He made sense of my stories and guided me when I got lost along the way.

So all I'm saying is, never give up on a dream, and if you do, find someone who believes in you – and, in my case, someone who can also spell. Thank you, Caleb, for helping me to achieve something beyond my dreams. We did it!

1

Nanny Downer and Nanny Twinkle

I've never been backward in coming forward, if you know what I mean. I've always been able to express myself and get my point across in any way necessary. I suppose I get that from my mum Pat – or Patricia Pamela Spence, to give you her full title. One of my strongest memories of Mum is that she never held back from expressing herself – if she had anything to say, she would just say it, especially when it concerned us kids. Pat was fiercely protective of us when we were growing up – not that she thought we were angels; by no means. There's me, who you know, otherwise you wouldn't be reading this little book; my sister Rennie is the eldest, then there are 11 months between her and Tania; then I am followed by the youngest girl, Kelly.

Mum had Rennie, Tania and me in the space of three years, and after the birth of each one of us she had a nervous breakdown. It's not that we were bad babies, you understand – it's just the family genes. I have never had a nervous breakdown, but I have been on the edge of one all my life! We'll get to that later in the book – the panic attacks and the hypochondria. It's really a wonder that I'm still alive, as I've had every disease under the sun. I'm a walking miracle.

Thinking about it, considering Dad worked two jobs day and night when we were babies, he must have come home just to do the deed with Mum. I think I must take after him in that respect; it's a good thing I'm gay and don't procreate. Honestly, I would be fathering kids left, right and centre. I'm ready at the drop of a hat.

At this time my parents lived with us three children in a two-bedroom maisonette called Keyes House in Enfield, London – Ponders End, to be precise. No wonder Mum had a nervous breakdown after each birth. Did I mention that she had her first child when she was just 17? And each one of us was a home birth.

I was born at 12.01 exactly. There's a story behind this that Dad always tries to tell, but Mum always chips in with her penny's worth. I was born on 6 April 1969, and before you try to work it out, yes, I do look good for my age. You can figure it out – I was always crap at maths.

I don't know if this still happens – I don't have any kids, so I'm not up on this kind of thing, but never say never. If I were born on 5 April, Dad would have received some kind of tax rebate. As you can imagine, what with having a young family, already with two toddlers, and only 11 months between them, Dad was practically trying to pull me out so that he could claim his rebate. While Mum lay there scream-ing in labour, Dad was shouting at her like she was some thoroughbred about to win the Grand National.

'*Go on girl, you can do it, push, push, get it out!*'

I don't think you'd get a thoroughbred in a council flat – you wouldn't fit them in, all that straw and hay, but anyway.

So, she's pushing and he's shouting – *'Push, shout, push, shout!'* – and in the middle of all this Dad's begging the midwife that if I came out on the sixth, could she backdate me to the fifth? The midwife, a large West Indian lady, who, even though I've never met her, I like to think of as my second mum, firmly replied no. So Dad thought, the direct approach isn't working. Try and charm her, ask her about her family, her husband, children, their names – anything he could think of to get me signed off for the fifth.

Being the bright spark that Dad is (not), he decided that he would name me after the midwife's husband, having known her only two hours. He figured this would convince her to backdate my date of birth. She was very flattered, apparently, but her professionalism didn't wane. I finally came out, as I said, at 12.01, a breech birth with the umbilical cord wrapped around my neck like a feather boa. I must have been doing a show in there. I'll perform for anyone and anything, intestines, kidneys – an audience is an audience. Ever the ultimate professional, like the midwife, I wasn't about to compromise my integrity by arriving early on the stage.

By now Mum had collapsed with exhaustion but Dad, undeterred, was still trying to work his charm on the midwife, who was busy trying to save me from strangling myself with my umbilical boa.

'So, can we put that as the fifth then?'

He thought it was like delivering Coca-Cola, which was his second job – you could backdate the invoice. Well, no, the midwife was having none of it. The sixth it was, my name had been declared – Louis.

Or it would have been, if Dad could spell. He was the one who registered my name, and I ended up with an 'e' instead of an 's'. Mind you, if I'd had both, I would have been Louise, which I could have worked, and I have actually, many a time. Well, thank Kylie, I should be so lucky, lucky, lucky, the midwife's husband's name wasn't Alfred. I don't think I could have worked that. Alfreda, Alfrena? No, it just doesn't work. In fact, I love my name, and I'm glad that Dad made the lucky mistake with the 'e', by choosing a letter I could actually pronounce. With my lisp, being born on the sixth of the fourth, '69 is enough of a challenge. It's far more unique, and it makes me feel special; I know what you're thinking, I *am* special. Special needs – I do have some of those, but I'll get to that soon.

I REMEMBER crawling on the concrete outside the maisonettes, where there was a lingering smell of stale wee. Maybe that's why I have an obsession with clean toilets now. I always make sure I don't sprinkle when I tinkle; I'm always a sweetie and wipe the seatie. I think having three sisters in the house probably had something to do with that as well.

The four of us kids used to share the bathwater. Once, after a trip to the seaside where I collected some shells, I took a wee in my little shells while I was in the bath. I thought it was OK because I was using the shells, but my sisters were not happy to be bathing in my piss. Another memory I have of my time in Keyes House is of crawling into the flat of a neighbour who had purple walls and a black leather sofa in

My first memories of Braintree are of bright sunshine and open space, with fields going on forever. I had never seen so many trees – the only ones I could remember from Ponders End were in the middle of a roundabout. Thinking back, they were not even trees, they were just bushes. I remember that, even though I didn't understand the meaning of the word posh at the age of three. I think if I did, the new house would have been it. I knew things were about to change, I could smell it along with the shit in the air.

Remembering our earlier life in Ponders End, I'm sure my parents argued neither more nor less than any other parents. With Mum's nervous breakdowns and Dad working every hour God sent, being in a one-bedroom maisonette with three screaming kids would put any relationship under pressure.

I remember once when the pressure got too much and it all exploded. We had popped round to Nan and Grandad Twinkle at Christmas.

Dad had bought Mum a beautiful chocolate-brown, full-length leather coat, with a split up the back and a fur collar. Mum loved it. She had bought Dad a lovely watch with a black leather strap – I say leather but knowing Mum, it was probably a bit of PVC, but it's the thought, isn't it? There we were, in the pissy lift on our way up to the sixteenth floor ... The three of us kids were modelling suede and sheepskin jackets. My sheepskin was white and my sisters' was pink. I wasn't happy about it – I also wanted pink sheepskin – but what's a budding gay to do when he can't make himself understood at the tender age of three?

1st floor. Ping! 2nd floor. By the 3rd floor the argument had started, but don't ask me what that was about. By the time we reached the 6th floor it was in full swing.

Me, with my dad, modelling a sheepskin and suede bomber
jacket with a lovely piece of costume jewellery to boot!

10th floor, Mum was trying to get Dad's watch off his wrist and I don't think it was because she wanted to know the time.

12th floor, Dad had taken off the watch and thrown it on the floor.

13th floor, Dad had ripped Mum's coat off her back.

14th floor, Dad had torn the coat in half.

15th floor, Mum stamped on Dad's bright new watch.

Ping! 16th floor, doors opened and there was Nanny Twinkle waiting to meet us, none the wiser about the antics that had been going on between floors 3 and 16.

IT'S FUNNY, isn't it, how everyone's Nan and Grandad seem to have certain names? Nanny Twinkle, Nanny Downer or Irish Nanny as we called her was an absolute treat. She literally made us piss our pants. Then there was Nanny Lock, because she lived down by Enfield Lock. Nanny Twinkle was Nanny Twinkle because she had a Yorkshire terrier called Twinkle, whom we all hated. It was like a little rat with a bow in its hair; it bit our ankles without fail whenever we visited.

Nanny Twinkle was as deaf as a blinking dodo so she would never hear us screaming and Grandad Twinkle would just growl back at the dog. He was a stern little man, Grandad Twinkle. In fact, he also had a talent – the complete opposite of mine and a little bit rougher. In his day he was a champion flyweight boxer. In fact, he was third best in the world. We didn't really have much to chat about, he and I, when I was a child. I only liked to visit them for the 50p that Nanny Twinkle would give us out of her teapot when we left.

Grandad Twinkle knocking them out.

Nanny Twinkle was a tall lady, so we can safely say that I didn't get any of her genes. She was a lovely woman who used to make all her own clothes. When Grandad wasn't looking I would try to get on to her Singer sewing machine, to run up a costume or two out of her old doilies. She always had a lovely purple rinse – not always the same shade, but she was way ahead of Gaga.

Then there was Nanny Lock, who was my great nan – she was Mum's nan. She was pretty amazing, I must say. At age 90, she was still getting on the bus going into Enfield Town to do all her own shopping. You could guarantee without fail that every time we turned up to visit, she would have rock cakes ready. And I do mean rock – I think they were left over from the last time we visited. She would give us a nice glass of R Whites lemonade, but don't ask me why, she would always put a teaspoon full of sugar in it. This would take away the fizz and made it taste like syrup water.

She was the sweetest old lady, always so generous and giving, and actually gave Nanny Twinkle a run for her money with her rinse. While Nanny Twinkle was working purple, Nanny Lock would work orange and white – white roots, orange at the ends.

She topped Nanny Twinkle on the old lady scale with a slight smell of stale wee that trailed her as she passed by in her stretch polyester pants. To top it all, her crowning glory was her knitted-lady toilet-roll covers. They were white and she must have modelled them on herself, as they all had red hair. She knitted them herself – there's someone who was ahead of the pack with self-branding. Had the opportunity been available, she might have been selling them in Liberty's – who knows? Maybe I'll have a word with them.

Then there was Grandad Lock, who I think must have been 95 then. He didn't say much – he was a horse messenger during the war, taking messages across enemy lines. At least, that's what we were told. That's how he got his leg blown off, and he had a wooden leg. We always used to laugh at him – he had smoked from the age of five to the day he died. He always had a fag in his mouth. Us kids used to wait for him to get to the end of his cigarette, which he smoked right down to the filter, and the end would fall on his wooden leg and burn a hole in his trousers – they ended up looking like a colander. He would stick his tongue out, take the filter and chew it and swallow it. No word of a lie, we all used to laugh at this!

NOW ON to Nanny Downer, or Irish Nanny. We didn't know her very well, only during the last five years of her life. She left my grandad and lost all contact with her family. I don't know all the reasons behind it, but even though Grandad Downer was wonderful with all us grandchildren, he was apparently very strict with Mum and her siblings, and could be quite heavy-handed with my nan so as soon as the youngest child, Uncle Glen, was old enough to fend for himself, Nanny Downer left to live a life of her own. She cut off contact with her family in case Grandad would find her and make her life a misery again.

But one day Mum got a phone call from the hospital to tell her that Nanny Downer was unwell. She had often spoken fondly of Nanny Downer, but us kids had never met her. When she got off the phone to the hospital, I could tell she was upset.

She said to Dad, 'We've *got* to go, we've *got* to go.' There was a sense of urgency in her voice and it bothered me to see her looking so vulnerable and frightened. To me she had always seemed invincible.

Dad said, 'What is it, Pat? What's the matter?'

Mum was starting to cry now. 'It's my Mum, it's my Mum! She's in the hospital and there's something wrong with her blood. I don't know, I couldn't take it in. I can't believe it, after all these years of trying to find her. Now I've found her and they say she might die.'

Dad was not the most articulate person and he always left the talking to Mum in most situations. He put his arms around her and hugged her tightly. 'She's not going to die, Pat, she's not. It's going to be alright.'

I looked at Dad and felt a great deal of love for him then, for protecting Mum. She was my world and he was looking after her.

At this point, Mum had had no contact with Nanny Downer for about 10 years. As you can imagine, it was a bittersweet moment. She was happy to be in touch with her mum after all these years, but worried about the circumstances under which they had regained contact. The doctors at the hospital told Mum that Nanny Downer had leukaemia and didn't have long to live. Literally from one day to the next, having never known her, Nanny Downer was suddenly living with us at home.

Even though we only knew her for a short period, she had a great impact on our lives, especially mine. Although she was unwell she was always full of energy, telling wonderful jokes and always laughing and smiling. She had a husky Belfast accent and was a great storyteller. I don't think all the stories she told us were true, but they were wonderful.

She had 22 brothers and sisters. Only 17 of them lived: I say 'only' – she used to tell us that they were so poor growing up, that she and her identical twin, Aggie (who died two years earlier of the same disease), used to knock on the doors of the rich in Belfast. They would pretend that Aggie was blind and that they were collecting money for blind charities, until one day they knocked on a door. The person who answered asked if they had a licence to collect money and, as Nanny Downer said, you've never seen a blind person run so

fast. She said it was like someone had put a rocket up Aggie's arse and lit it. When Frank Carson says, 'It's the way you tell 'em', it certainly is. With her heavy accent and rolling laugh, it was definitely the way she told her stories that had us in fits of laughter.

There was another time when Mum and Dad went on holiday for a week and Nanny Downer was left in charge. I know what you're thinking, it was irresponsible of my parents to leave a dying old lady in charge of three young kids, and maybe it was. But it was one of the best weeks of our lives and I still laugh about it now with my sisters. That was it – as soon as the door was shut and Mum and Dad were on their way, Nanny Downer (who was a recovering alcoholic, who never recovered), had me wheel her to the top of the road to Londis to get her Special Brew.

Being old and sweet-looking, in a wheelchair and with CCTV not being such a big thing then, filling up your wheelchair with Special Brew under your crocheted blanket and leaving the store without paying was quite an easy thing to do. What with me being a minor, and I don't suppose anyone was prepared to check an old lady dying of leukaemia, it was a win–win situation.

We were set up for the week: Nan had her Special Brew and she agreed we didn't have to go to school and wrote each of us a letter to take to our teachers. We had come down with a terrible bug – I think it was called shoplifting. She would have given Fagin a run for his money.

All of our friends came over to visit and we had what you might call an early rave. I had my first glass of cider and kissed a girl, and I haven't touched either since. I had a puff of Nan's JPS Special, the long ones with the extra bit of nicotine to kill you off, as she was always joking. Our time together was short, but it was a special bond that we developed with her and the jokes still have us laughing to this day. I often wish that she was still alive because I know that, now I am grown up, she would definitely have been one of my best friends as well as a special nan.

Nanny Downer could laugh even when the situation was beyond a joke. At this time Mum was working at a fashion store called Foxy Lady in Braintree town, yet another of her part-time jobs. It sold one-off designer outfits, but no designer you would have heard of. No Christian Dior here, maybe some Christine DeLor – you know the type I mean.

Mum thought it would be nice for Nanny Downer to sit in the garden for a couple of hours one sunny day while she popped off to do a shift at Foxy Lady. As it was a Saturday, I went with Mum to help her dress the shop. I say 'dress the shop', but I was dressing myself most of the time. It was the time of *Dynasty* – coat dresses and shoulder pads. I looked a treat!

We left Nanny Downer sitting in the garden in her wheelchair with a can of Special Brew that I had slipped under her blanket for her. I think Mum probably knew it was there, even though she didn't approve, but Nanny Downer had given me the sign. She held up an imaginary can and knocked it back and forth in her hand. She used to hide the cans in her cupboard, which was more than just a cupboard but I'll get to that later.

We wheeled her to a corner of the garden, where there was just the right amount of sunshine and shade, and she was modelling one of her synthetic blue flowery dresses, one of those that would melt if you lit a match anywhere near it.

She also had one in pink and another in yellow, but that Saturday she was working the blue dress and a perky straw hat in her wheelchair.

As we left, Mum asked, 'Are you alright, Mum? Do you need anything?'

'I'm alright, Patsy, be off with you. Go to work.'

I think she couldn't wait for us to leave so she could neck her Special Brew and she gave me a conspiratorial wink as I waved goodbye. As we turned out the back gate I heard the click and 'psshhht' as she opened her can of Brew.

What started off as a beautiful summer's day when we left Nanny Downer in the garden quickly changed with a torrential storm while Mum and I were at Foxy Lady. But we thought nothing of it, she was sorting out stock and I was practising my window-dressing skills.

When we arrived home and walked into the garden after Mum's shift, there was Nanny Downer in the same position we had left her. She did not have the strength or the ability to wheel herself around in her wheelchair and she looked like a drowned rat. She had been caught in the downpour and was soaked through. Her straw hat had collapsed around her face, while her synthetic dress collected rainwater in little puddles in her lap.

Mum gasped in horror.

'Oh, Mum, I'm so sorry, I'm so sorry! I forgot we left you out here! Are you alright?'

Nanny Downer replied in her broad Belfast accent, 'Do *I* fucking *look* alright, Patsy? Look at me! I've got a dress I could swim in and half of my face is burnt.' She was sunburnt on half her body – we had strategically left her in the sun to burn on the diagonal. Her glasses had slid to the end of her nose and they were misty, with beads of water obscuring her vision.

'What are you trying to do, kill an old lady?' At this point she burst into a heavy belly laugh, which Mum and I caught and joined in with.

Whenever Nanny Downer laughed and tried to speak at the same time, she might as well have been speaking Swahili to the rest of us. Only Mum and my aunties could under-stand her at that point – it's something you had to be brought up with. Her laughter was powerful and rich, and swept everyone along with it: her life was full of such extremes and her laughter seemed to sit comfortably with the tragedy that had marked much of it.

Thank God Nanny Downer got back in touch with us because the holiday before, when Mum and Dad went off to one of the Costas on an all-inclusive, we were sent to bleeding Christian camp for a week. I say a week, but the whole process took a lot longer. You see, to go to Christian camp, you had to go to Sunday School and it's not as if you could just pop in the week before. Oh no, I don't know exactly how long you had to go before, but I know that we went for a whole year.

Dad is an atheist, Mum isn't bothered either way, and not one of us had been christened. You can imagine what that would have been like, with Dad's spelling. Christ knows what names we would have ended up with. But in fairness to Mum and Dad, half the Goldingham estate was at Christian club, or Sunday school, or whatever they called it back then. All the parents had clocked on to the fact that they could get a week away from the kids and wouldn't have to pay for the holiday.

No, *we* had to pay for it! Every Sunday morning, pretend-ing we were interested in the Bible, just because we were going to get a free holiday. In saying that, we all had a lot of fun at Sunday School and on our free camping – yes, camping – holiday. Mind you, everything with me was camp; I didn't need a tent and five other boys to share it with, but that's what we got.

There were no mixed tents there – family or not, we were strictly segregated. There was a lot of singing around the camp fire too – I still remember one of the songs:

> *No, you never get to heaven,*
> *In a baked bean tin,*
> *No, you never get to heaven,*
> *In a baked bean tin,*
> *No, you never get to heaven in a baked bean tin,*
> *'Cos a baked bean tin has got baked beans in.*

We used to sing the same song about a Playtex bra as well. It didn't make much sense to me then and it still doesn't now.

Even at that age, it wasn't what I would have called glamorous. Not that I had experienced true glamour back then, but I had been to Butlin's. It was at Butlin's that I won my first talent competition, unaware that I had entered it. I just heard the music and I followed it, wandering off from my parents into the ballroom. I started doing my high kicks, my cartwheels and my roly-polies.

I was only about five and when Mum and Dad finally found me, along with five Redcoats and the camp security, Mum was beside herself and close to having another one of her nervous breakdowns. It was something she eventually got used to: wherever there was music and a crowd, I could always be found in the middle of the action, mincing like a maniac.

2
Me and Mr Whippy

We made so many new friends when we arrived in Braintree! Next door to us lived the Sherlocks – Jonathan, Kim, Kerry, Julia, Simon and Tara. Then the Joneses at number three – Sharon, Michelle, Paul and Wayne. Then Gary Smith, just around the back, with his older brother Smudger (everyone fancied him). Don't get me wrong, he was cute, but I never fancied him. At the tender age of five, I had a thing for Mr Whippy, the ice-cream man. Don't ask me why – maybe it's because he gave me extra sauce and nuts on my 99 ice-cream, but there was something about him that captivated me.

Whenever his ice-cream van was around, I would have to go and speak to him, even if Mum couldn't afford to buy me an ice-cream that evening. He always made me feel special and spoke to me as an adult, not the little kid I was. He was very gentle and kind – there was nothing untoward with Mr Whippy. Now, I don't know if this was possible, but I fancied him. Yes, at five years old, I think I fancied Mr Whippy. Can you believe I never found out his name – my first love and I don't know his name! Maybe someone who knows Mr Whippy, who used to come to Goldingham Drive circa '75–'85, could let me know.

I can still see his face now: he had beautiful, thick, jet-black shiny hair, with a side parting and he was always perfectly groomed. Even though he was freshly shaved, he still had that shadow – you know what I mean, that type. He had the deepest chocolate-brown eyes and the longest lashes I had ever seen on a man. Believe me, I'd seen some lashes – you should have seen some of the falsies Mum used to wear in the Seventies. Whenever she was out, I would have them on more than once.

Anyway, back to Mr Whippy, whose lips were soft and full; he had the most beautiful smile and white teeth that made the five-year-old me melt. A five-year-old who didn't even know the word gay, so don't talk to me about nature and nurture. Let's get one thing straight – I came screaming out of that womb, high kicking and dancing.

I SUPPOSE there were advantages to being the only boy, even though Dad jokes now and says he had four girls. Having your own bedroom in a three-bedroom house, with two sisters in one and your parents in the other is great when you are a teenager: you can shut the door and knock one out whenever you want.

But at five years old, when I was used to sharing a room with my two older sisters, Rennie and Tania, and having someone to speak to, or just knowing someone was there when I went to sleep, I felt lonely and afraid of the dark in my own room. I remember the silence, which we never had in London, where I was used to the sound of cars and people.

I slept in an MFI box-bed – I say box-bed, but I ended up sleeping in the drawers. It was one of those beds that had the chest of drawers underneath, with a bit of cheap plywood separating the mattress from the drawers, so I fell straight through and ended up in the top drawer alongside my Spiderman and Superman polyester pants. I remember literally sweating my bollocks off in those pants and if you didn't shake and got a dribble of wee in them, they would keep the smell. There I am, back on wee again! Let's get off the wee and back on to poor, poor, lonely me, alone at night in my room. I'll tell you what I used to do – I would climb out of bed (or my top drawer) and crawl on all-fours to my sisters' room next door to mine, holding my breath so they wouldn't hear me breathe.

This was Tania and Rennie, as Kelly hadn't arrived yet. When Kelly arrived, my relationship with Mum changed – and not for the better, in my eyes. I used to love the times when Mum and I were together on our own. I don't know if everyone feels like this, but I can remember at a young age what it was like to have to share her with the rest of the family. I loved it when my sisters went to school and Dad went to work, and it was just Mum and me left in the house, after I had been to playschool. Rennie and Tania were already doing full days at infant school.

I remember following her around wherever she went, and I loved sitting and watching her putting on her make-up. Mum always made an effort – she never left the house without doing her hair and her make-up. To me, she was the most

beautiful woman ever. I used to compare her to other women, even at that young age, and thinking that they were not the same as my mum – no make-up, hair not done. When she would pick me up from playschool, at Goldingham Hall, about two minutes from home, to me she would stand out from the other mums because she always looked so good.

I was very proud to see Mum every day after playschool, then we would go home and she would make lunch. We sat and talked – don't ask me what about – we would just talk. Then we would lay on the sofa together in spoons and watch the afternoon film or *The Sullivans*. I remember that feeling of security without cares, of complete and total safety. That disappears soon enough and I am glad that I still have those memories.

I can clearly remember when that feeling disappeared. It was when my sister Kelly arrived. I was a bit pissed off when she came along, because I was used to getting all the attention. But when she was born, all I got was a packet of fruit pastilles from my Auntie Maureen and no more spooning on the sofa. As you can imagine, someone like me needs a lot of attention but what chance did I have against a screaming baby? None. I can remember feeling a bit lost and lonely: my sisters had each other, Mum and Dad had each other, and who did I have? No-one. All I had was my MFI bed and my first panic attack.

Rennie, my oldest sister, would make me sit and tickle her feet until we both fell asleep. There were many nights when I ended up asleep at the foot of her bed and many more nights when I was woken by a loud Beep-Beep-Beep, the sound of Tania's bedwetting alarm. You see, she had a weak bladder and couldn't keep it in; as soon as she started

Me, Kelly and Rennie at the beach on one of our holidays.

to wee the bed, the wee would hit a metal mesh underneath the plastic sheet beneath her bed sheet. Every time she moved in the bed, it sounded like she was crushing a plastic bag.

The alarm would wake Mum, who would put me back in my bed, and I would go back to sleep feeling less lonely, until the next night when it would all be repeated. This continued until I was about 25. No, I'm lying – Tania only wet the bed until the age of 19.

Mum was an absolute clean freak – most families wake up in the morning to the smell of toast, we woke up to the smell of disinfectant. If cleanliness is next to godliness, then bleach was her holy water.

When we went downstairs each morning before school, Dad would already have left for work. At this time he was working on building sites – he was known for the large number of bricks he could carry on his hod.

We had to sit on the sofa in the living room. Nanny Downer would be in the cupboard on her commode, farting away while we all laughed. She would shout at us from inside the cupboard, 'What are you laughing at out there?'

Then she would shout at Mum, 'Patsy, Patsy, what are they laughing at out there?'

Only Nanny Downer called Mum 'Patsy'. The more we laughed, the more Nanny Downer laughed, and the more she farted. It was not her fault, it was caused by the medication she was on, bless her.

Why was Nanny Downer in the cupboard on her commode? You might well ask. Her illness had left her too weak to walk and she could not get up and down the stairs. So, Dad decorated the shoe-and-coat cupboard downstairs, where we also kept the Hoover. He gave it a lick of paint and put some pictures on the wall, with a nice floral border in the middle.

Fortunately, Nanny Downer didn't have to stay in the cupboard too long. She eventually got a warden-controlled flat around the corner, with a fully fitted loo, and we got our cupboard back. The shoes and Hoover had never had it so good – a cupboard fit for a commode!

Anyway, back to my mum's cleaning regime. We were on the sofa because the kitchen floor would be wet from a good old scrub. There would be Shake'n'Vac all over the three-tone shagpile carpet, which was brown and cream with black flecks. This accompanied our orange leather sofa and mahogany-stained wood panelling, which Mum had sprayed with Mr Sheen, ready to be wiped down. The smoked-glass mirrored tiles on the walls would also be cleaned with vinegar water to bring out their shine.

Only when the kitchen floor was dry and we had been sufficiently intoxicated with the fumes of every cleaning product she could find a surface for, were we allowed to sit down for breakfast, which had to be a rushed affair.

No sooner had Mum put the plate down than she was taking it back to wash, dry and put away. While my two sisters were at school and I was at playschool, Mum would pop off to Bourne's pie factory, where everyone in the town seemed to work, to do a quick shift. She was that manic and obsessed with cleanliness that she couldn't leave the house without it looking as though no-one lived there.

This was not a once-a-week event, it was an everyday occurrence. Sometimes my sisters and I wonder why we have the habits we do, such as our neurotic addiction to cleanliness. Don't get me started on the hypochondria and panic attacks. No, actually, *do* – we may as well start that here, because it's an ongoing process that will keep popping up throughout this book, as it pops up throughout my life.

When we were kids, Mum would take us all to the doctor's if one of us was ill and she would claim that we were all ill. She would say, yes, they've got a sore throat – he's still got it, she's getting it – even if we didn't. We would all be put on penicillin – I don't know if people have penicillin any more, do they? I remember it had to be kept in the fridge; it was milky white in colour and I remember enjoying the taste of it. We used to have it that often, we didn't need Mum to supervise us with the dosage: we knew exactly how much to take.

Honestly, when I was 12, I thought I had a womb and was about to start my period because I just did everything my sisters did. I'm so glad they used towels when they started and not tampons, otherwise I would have really been in trouble.

As I said, I did everything my sisters did, and that's how my dancing days started – they went dancing, I went dancing, and I just kept on dancing …

I don't think my sisters really wanted to go dancing. It was just that Mum wanted to get rid of all three of us on a Saturday morning so she could go shopping along with the rest of the town. Doreen Cliff School of Dance, at the Braintree Institute, must have been making a bloody fortune – when I say every kid in the town was there, they really were. Well, the girls and me.

Before I went to Doreen Cliff's School I was already doing my own thing. I was always loose – I could always do the splits, not technically correct, but my legs were quite rubbery. I can remember as clear as day lying on my front on our shagpile in front of the TV, getting high on the Shake'n'Vac that the vacuum cleaner couldn't quite reach.

I liked rocking back and forth on my front as I lay in front of the TV and before I knew it, my feet had gone over my head and I had one foot next to each ear. Mum freaked out – I think she thought I had snapped in half and you can imagine what must have been going through her mind. Penicillin wouldn't fix this one! But I just rolled out and was as right as rain.

So, when I got to Doreen Cliff's I enjoyed putting myself in a ball in acro class. For anyone who doesn't know what that is, it's a bit like contortion. Well, it was at Doreen Cliff's

School. She would bend you into any shape she wanted and of course she loved me. A boy with that facility! I was already grabbing attention at age five.

It didn't take me long to get into the swing of things at Doreen Cliff's – as soon as I got a pair of Lycra tights, that was it. I loved it and I couldn't wait for Saturday mornings. I remember I would wake up before the bleach had hit the kitchen floor, with my bag packed and ready to go.

Now, the Braintree Institute isn't really that big. I only went back there a few months ago as Doreen was retiring after 45 years, but I remember when I was five how grand it all seemed. The main hall had a stage with big red curtains, which was only for end-of-year shows.

Our classes were held upstairs, in dusty, cold rooms with grey lino floors. Remembering the smell of the cold concrete walls and the plastic lino still makes me smile now. As soon as I walked through the doors I felt happy and excited, and I couldn't wait to continue what we had been doing the week before.

I loved the work we did and I was eager to progress. Early on I learned that if you practise, you can improve, and I did – I got better, week after week. I was stimulated and felt that it was for a reason, even though I didn't know what the reason was. I didn't have to try, it just happened. I could perform any task I was set and I had no idea at the time that this would be my career.

In contrast, I remember I hated my first day at primary school and every day after, along with anything academic. I know some people look back and say schooldays were the best days of their lives, but the academic side used to make me physically sick.

I remember one day when I was in junior school, aged about nine, I jumped over the school fence and went home. When Mum saw me, she asked me what I was doing at home. I burst into tears and told her that I didn't like school and I didn't want to go back. She calmly gave me a lolly and listened to me, before sending me back to school: she made the situation less traumatic than it might have felt because she didn't make a big hoo-ha about it.

Talking about sweets, our mum bought us sweets every evening, which she would then leave behind the kettle. How random is that? Each night we would come home and check behind the kettle to see what sweets we had, and she never forgot, even though, like Dad, she was holding down two jobs. As you get older you can forget how amazing your parents were. Anyway, back to me and my dancing.

Don't get me wrong, I used to like walking to school with my friends and coming home, as well as classes in country dancing and gymnastics in between, but that was about it.

All my school reports said, 'Louie could do better if he concentrated, if he tried harder.'

I suppose I could have tried harder, but how could I concentrate? I sat in class behind Trudie Francesconi, who had long, shiny dark brown hair which reached her waist. I used to imagine what it must be like to have hair that long. When she moved her head, her hair would follow a couple of beats later, and you could see your reflection in it when the sun shone on her hair.

During playtime while the boys were kicking balls around, you could find me brushing Trudie's hair in the playground. When I was finished, I would crown it with a daisy chain, which I had skilfully put together. I was known for my rose petal perfume and my daisy chains at John Ray Infants School.

None of the kids thought anything of it. I was just Louie, and even at that very young age, I had a big personality that could make people laugh. I think this prevented others from categorising me as anything but Louie. I had such confidence and I was never apologetic for who I was. My behaviour did not seem wrong and none of my friends seemed to think it was.

I often crowned myself Fairy Princess and sprayed myself with my home-made rosewater perfume. And I was very content with my daisy crowns until Nadine Leicester was crowned Braintree Carnival Princess. She brought her sparkling diamante tiara to school and I was dumbstruck: I had never seen anything so beautiful in my life. Even Trudie's shiny hair could not compete with the sparkle and shine of this real princess's tiara.

I *had* to have it. Nadine was not someone I played with much, even though she lived around the corner from me, next to Gary Smith – who I played with more often. But Nadine was soon to become one of my best friends. I started by brushing her hair at playtime. It was not like brushing Trudie's hair: Trudie had hair like satin and it was straight as spaghetti, but Nadine's hair had a slight curl. Her hair was also slightly coarse, with a few split ends. I had learned what split ends were from my sisters.

Nadine was not going to give up her crown easily. It took a lot of brushing and plaiting, and giving up my lunchbox treats of Milky Ways, Curly Wurlies, Blue Riband, and I lost count of how many packets of pickled onion Monster Munch.

But it was *so* worth it. The day had arrived! I went around to Nadine's house after school and there it was, in her bedroom on top of her chest of drawers. I was transfixed and before I knew it, I had it in my hands and placed it on my head. I was a princess, if only for a few seconds.

Nadine was having none of it. She snatched it from me and said she was going to tell her mum. In one sense, I was glad it was over: it meant no more giving away my lunch-box treats. If only I knew then what I know now – I did not need her tiara to be a princess! Look at me now, I'm the queen of Braintree!

I found school lessons uninspiring and boring compared to classes with Doreen Cliff, which filled me with so much joy. Where her classes seemed to finish too quickly, school seemed never-ending. I don't know how I learned to read and write – I never paid any attention in class. It must have been a purely unconscious process. I suppose it was lucky I wasn't conscious. Who knows, I might have studied and ended up running a corporation or country somewhere, in Lycra, no doubt. No, let's keep it real: that would never have happened.

But I lie – I do remember learning something at school, with Mrs Pye, when I was about six. I learned how to tie my shoelaces in a double bow; we practised on a big cardboard boot.

My attitude to school did not change throughout junior school and continued into my first year of senior school, when I decided to try and get into Italia Conti in London, with the help of Doreen Cliff.

I REMEMBER the first show we ever did at Doreen Cliff's School, on the big stage with the red curtains. I played a chicken and a hula boy, and the girls were all hula girls. We rehearsed and rehearsed and rehearsed – Doreen was very tough, even with five-year-olds. She made sure everything was perfect for the big night. And everything *was* perfect – my parents had even bought me a little gold signet ring in celebration. But could they get me on that stage? Neither for love nor a gold signet ring! My chicken was not clucking that evening.

I had a fear I had not experienced before; not even lonely nights in my MFI bed could compare to this. I couldn't breathe, which might have been because the elastic around the chicken head was asphyxiating me. Whatever the reason, I did not want to go on stage. That was my only experience of stage fright. Lucky it happened then and not at a paying gig, but I didn't get the gold signet ring. I suspect they had only bought it to keep me out of Mum's jewellery box, with its beads and clip-ons.

I was worried after this no-show that Mum wouldn't allow me to go back to dance classes at Doreen Cliff's. I don't know what I would have done without those classes, because I felt complete when I was dancing – a bit of ballet, tap and disco. I did love a bit of disco – all that thrusting, all that Lycra. Of course she let me go back – she wanted to keep her Saturday mornings free.

I started to take my exams at Doreen Cliff's in acro, disco, tap and modern. I always received Honours for acro and disco, and I loved the exams because it meant I would have to get new costumes. One of my favourite costumes was an electric blue all-in-one Lycra catsuit with stirrups. Now, you could dress this up or down, depending on how you wanted it. Back in the disco days, elasticated sequins were all the rage, especially on armbands, anklebands, belts and head-bands. You could also have tinsel tassels, which is a mouthful for me, but it looked amazing when doing a disco spin. I loved sewing the tassels – give me a needle, thread and sequins and I'm in my element.

I remember coming home once to find Dad in my Lycra all-in-one, prancing around in front of the family, which they thought was very funny, but I was pissed off. I did not find it funny, at the age of seven, having spent ages sewing on my tinsel tassels, that he might stretch my all-in-one and ruin it. It was for seven-to nine-year-olds, not for 30! It was my life!

Dancing had been my life since the age of five and I lived for Saturday mornings, and Tuesdays and Wednesdays after school, when I would go to dance classes. My parents never had to wake me up or push me to attend dance classes – it was always my choice. I was never late for class and they never interfered or prevented me from attending.

EVEN THOUGH I loved going to Doreen Cliff School of Dance at the Braintree Institute, I knew that there wasn't enough for me to learn – I seemed to master whatever I was taught very quickly and if I didn't, I would work on it night and day until the next lesson. That was when my friend Yvonne O'Grady who lived at number five, by the park with the swings and roundabouts, told me about a new dance school that she was attending in a nearby village.

Yvonne and I use to attend trampolining classes after school when I wasn't dancing and I became North Essex champion. Sometimes we used to practise trampoline moves from a trampette on to crash mats and move on to the trampoline when we had perfected the move. Well, I thought I had perfected it, until I did the double-front summersault into a front drop and I didn't open up, but over-rotated, staying in a nice tight tuck.

Whenever I concentrated, I always had my tongue hanging out. Not really a good thing to do when you're on a trampoline doing a double-front tuck. When I landed, without opening out, my knee hit my chin, pushing my teeth through my tongue. Being the neurotic drama queen that I am, obviously I thought I was going to bleed to death, but I ended up with only four stitches and an even worse lisp than I started out with. Thank God I didn't get myself a job selling sausages, or I'd have been up shit creek without a paddle! Mind you, as I'd always had a lisp, I don't think anyone noticed much difference.

There was only one problem: apparently there was an age requirement for Dadina's school. It was 13, unlucky for some and very unlucky for me, considering I was only 11 going on 12. But by hook and by crook, by high kick and splits, I was determined to attend Dadina's School of Dance.

Yvonne had already been attending classes for about five weeks and she used to show me some of the dance moves that Dadina had taught her. Well, you could have blown me down with a feather when she showed me what she had been learning at Dadina's school! It was like what they did in *Fame*. How was I going to get there? How was I going to convince Dadina that even though I wasn't old enough, I should attend her school?

Dadina had started a dancing school in Little Bardfield, which was a village about six miles from Braintree, and I knew that I had to go. I didn't know Dadina, but I had seen her at school; she hadn't been there long but you really couldn't miss her. She was unlike all the other girls at school – she had an aura about her. Whenever I saw her leaving school to get into her mum's Rolls-Royce, it was like time slowed down. She was tall, Anglo-Asian, around 15/16 with thick, jet-black hair that bounced in rhythm when she walked. And what a walk she had – straight back, head held high, working Notley High School's drive like a Paris catwalk.

I asked Yvonne to put in a good word for me, which, being the lovely person she was, she did. I say lovely person, I told her otherwise I would tell all the boys in school that she wore brown towelling knickers with yellow piping, which came away from the seams. (One thing girls had worked out at an early age was when a boy was gay and they could take their leotards off without them trying to look at their budding boobs. You know the stage I mean, girls, when your tits look like a little witch's hat.) Yvonne, not wanting her towelling knickers exposed to the whole of Notley High School, agreed that she would have a word with Dadina.

I felt like I was being summoned! Dadina had agreed to meet me – the beautiful, goddess-like figure that I looked at in awe – obviously not a sexual awe but I can't help but love a beautiful woman, and Dadina certainly was this.

So, Yvonne told me during a lunch break to meet her and Dadina on the wall outside the Rose & Crown at 12.30, next door to the Londis where I used to nick Special Brew for Nanny Downer. Of course I said yes, even though there was a dilemma as I wasn't on the going-home-for-lunch list. I couldn't work out how I was going to get out of the school gates, past the dinner ladies. Believe me, they could be like the bleeding Gestapo.

Well, there was a God, because lucky for me on that day, the dinner ladies must have been having a meeting. Goody Two Shoes Phillipa Morris was on her own on tick-out duties; her farts probably didn't even smell, she thought she was that perfect, but she can't have been that perfect because I managed to shimmy my way past her while she was busy being the perfect prefect.

I was bang on time for my meeting outside the Rose & Crown, but to my utter disappointment there was no sign of Yvonne or Dadina. I could feel my heart sinking; first, there was the real chance that Mum was doing her shopping in the Londis next door. Secondly, I was worried about being caught outside the school when I wasn't allowed out and thirdly, my dreams of dancing like Leroy were slipping away.

But, hold on – was that the sound of cork shoes on concrete? It certainly was, and there she was – 5, 6, 7, 8, and walk, 6, 7, 8. There she was, with her perfect rhythm.

I was frightened, but excited and my stomach was turning as I watched her approach. What if she said I couldn't go to her classes? Perhaps I'd break down in tears – maybe that would work? It was an option that I was holding in the back of my mind if things didn't turn out well.

Before I knew it, there she was in front of me. She put her hand out and shook mine, and said, 'Hello, Louie, my name is Dadina. Very nice to meet you.'

She was so grown up, even though she wasn't quite 16.

'Yvonne tells me you would like to come to my dancing

I think you get what I mean when I say, 'Dadina didn't
look like any other girl at school.' Hello!

school.'

Once I had caught my breath and tried to be as composed as an 11 going on 12-year-old could be – shaking on the inside, strong on the outside – I replied, 'Yes, I would, please, thank you very much.'

'How old are you?'

I knew that the admission age was 13, so I said 13, but Yvonne, thinking she was being really cool because she was Dadina's new BF, said, 'No, you're not! You're only 11.'

Don't ask me where it came from, but I just shouted out, 'Well, at least I don't have brown towelling knickers, which are falling apart, and tits like a witch's hat!'

This made Dadina laugh out loud, and she said, 'I'll make an exception this time. You can come on Saturday and let me see how you dance.'

Well, if you can imagine me at 11 going on 12, five foot nothing, screaming at the top of my voice, 'Yes, yes, *yes*, I'll be there!' All those s's, and with my balls not having dropped, my voice was so high-pitched, I almost cracked the windows of the Rose & Crown.

WITH A hop, skip, a jump and a turn, a high kick, a cartwheel and a back flip, I made my way back to school. And that's not an exaggeration – I thought I would give Dadina a little preview of what I could do. I was determined there was no way she was going to turn me down. And she didn't.

That Saturday morning when I arrived at Little Bardfield Hall, a 26-bedroom mansion with a massive barn where Dadina held her dance lessons, I was a triumph. I was wearing my best Lycra all-in-one. It was a deep maroon, long-sleeved, with stirrup foot, a scalloped neck and low-cut back.

If you think that sounds a bit feminine, you are right: it was a girls' all-in-one, but they didn't have them for boys. They didn't even sell them, come to that, they had to order them in. All they sold was aerobics gear. When people say they've done aerobics and it's just like dancing, it's not at all, and neither is the attire. But the lady in the shop wouldn't order just one boys' unitard as she wouldn't get her discount and I was the only boy in the town interested in them. So I made do with a girls' one, which was nothing new to me, I was always in my sisters' old clothes.

I never had a problem carrying something off with a feminine touch and I still don't. So, back to me being a triumph. We started off with a nice slow warm-up and this wasn't disco or ISTD, which is a dance syllabus: this was called modern jazz, which is what they did in the *Fame* class on TV. I was feeling dizzy, I was that excited – I couldn't believe there was someone other than Lydia Grant (the *Fame* dance teacher played by Debbie Allen) who knew how to teach this style.

Once again, unlike my academic skills, I found it so easy. I didn't have to think about it; whatever she taught, I followed with ease and I knew she could see it: I could see the smile on her face. I didn't see any smiles on Donna Forrester or Yvonne O'Grady's faces. They were her star pupils, until I arrived, and they were not happy. But hey, this was my destiny and no-one was going to mess with it – and they didn't.

At the end of the class, Dadina sat down with us and told everyone how well I did, and how lovely it was to see someone with so much potential, especially a boy. She then told me that she would be happy to teach me and so that was the start of a wonderful friendship and a great learning experience.

FOR THE next year, as well as attending Doreen Cliff's classes during the week, I would attend classes with Dadina every Friday night after school and stay overnight. At first this frightened the life out of me: the house was so big and so old, I was far too scared to sleep in a room on my own, as was Yvonne, who also used to come over on a Friday night so we would sleep in Dadina's bedroom. Well, I say bedroom – you could have fitted my box-room in it a hundred times. It was massive, with a walk-in wardrobe filled to the brim, may I add. The room was divided in two sections by wooden beams that creaked in the night.

Yvonne and Dadina slept at one end of the room and I slept at the other end on a massive cushion on the floor, under a lot of blankets. The weight of the blankets on me made me feel less scared, don't ask me why. There was no way I'd be going for a wee in the middle of the night! The bathroom was a mile down the corridor and I would have pissed my pants before I got there, I was that frightened.

Saturdays became the highlight of my life. I know that may sound a bit dramatic, but it's true. Dadina had been taught by various teachers in London and her teaching style was very strict and disciplined. It was not like Doreen Cliff's, where there were a large number of students of varying levels and abilities. Dadina expected us to be as disciplined as she was and she wanted to see progress in us. If your *développé* started at 45 degrees, the next week she would want it higher, and even higher the week after that, until it was up around your ears. If you did one turn, she wanted two; if you did two, she wanted three, and so on and so on.

But the most wonderful thing for me was the technical ability that I was developing under her teaching; it gave me the freedom to express myself through the music when I danced. This was a new and wonderful experience that has never left me.

In Dadina's barn I experienced what it was to dance to a piece of music and feel truly at one with it. It was, and is for me, the most wonderful feeling as a dancer: melting together with the music. It is like time stands still and the world has stopped moving; it's a magical feeling and one that I feel blessed to have.

4
Italia Conti

In spite of Dad having pranced about in my Lycra, all could be forgiven, considering the pains he took to try and get me into the Italia Conti Stage School in London. The daughter of one of Doreen's friends, who worked as a dinner lady at Italia Conti, was a student there. Because I was advancing quickly through Doreen's school, her friend offered to try and get me an audition at Italia Conti. Even though it cost an arm and a leg, there were people queuing up to get their children into the school.

I waited for the post every morning after requesting a prospectus from Italia Conti and a week later, bang! There it was, in a big white envelope, with the Italia Conti stamp on it. It felt as if all my birthdays had come at once.

Once my parents opened it and started to read, the look on their faces became very serious. I was very anxious watching them, knowing only they could make my dream come true. I thought it was going to be easy – I would get the prospectus, do the audition and start.

At age 12 I did not think about the financial implications, or the fact that I had three sisters and my parents were each working two jobs. I truly felt my life would be over if I could not get into Italia Conti. I would have done anything for this opportunity and I felt trapped within myself. I knew I had so much more to give, and so much more to explore, but I could not explore it in Braintree. It was now or never, and I knew that if I went to Italia Conti, it would change my life.

My parents explained that it would cost a lot of money that they did not have, that they would have to get money from the bank. I had to be one hundred per cent sure that this was what I wanted to do; I might even have to live away from home. If I lived at home, I would have to get an early train each morning and arrive home late in the evenings. They pointed out that there would no longer be time to play with my friends and that the whole family would have to make sacrifices for this. My sisters might have to miss out on school trips, birthdays and all the things you take for granted as a child.

But as you can imagine, in 1982, at 12 years old, all I could think of was going to this school that I imagined to be like the TV show *Fame*. I was going to be the next Leroy, apart from the fact that I was 12, white, gay and had a lisp. In my mind I couldn't see any reason why I couldn't be black with tight, toned thighs and perfect cane-rows in my hair. That was my inspiration, I had not seen dance like that before in my life. When I watched Leroy (I know it's not his real name) and the rest of the cast of *Fame* dancing, I knew that was how I was born to dance: I knew that burning passion inside me had to be released.

I know it may sound selfish, but I did not care whether my sisters went on school trips, or couldn't get a pair of pipeline jeans. (For those of you who don't know what pipeline jeans are, they were skin-tight with a slight bit of stretch and piping down the outside of the leg. They were available in many different colours and gave a lovely line, which was great for lengthening the leg. I have always loved a good line and a bit of length.)

This feeling was so strong, I couldn't let what Mum and Dad were telling me take my dream away. Nothing, and no-one, was going to stand in my way: I knew even then that I had to audition, otherwise I would never have been able to forgive myself or my parents if they stopped me from pursuing my dream. There are certain things in your life that you know are right, a feeling so strong that you don't have to question it. There are other times where you dither and nothing comes of it. I don't think I'm special, I think it comes to us all in different forms, for different things.

For the first time that I could remember, my parents treated me as a grown-up when they spoke to me about the process. They knew how important it was to me and wanted me to understand how difficult it was going to be financially if I passed the audition. I think there was a part of them that wanted me to say that I didn't really want to go, but they could both see that this was not just a fad that I had decided on lightly.

So, regardless of whether Mum and Dad were going to pay, in my head I was already there. I say already there, I would still have to get through the audition process. As I said, everything in dance came easy to me: I didn't have to think about it but now I was starting to poop my pants a little because not only did I have to dance, but I also had to sing and act.

Now, the acting I didn't think I'd have a problem with, until I read that it had to be a piece of Shakespeare. Starting off with an 'S' was not a good sign and as for singing, I'd never tried it, just 'Happy Birthday' at the odd party. So that was my song choice, 'Happy Birthday', everyone knows it. It's good to have something everyone can sing along to. I also didn't dare to ask my parents for more money for singing lessons.

Nothing is for free in this world, is it? Well, saying that, now I get a lot of things for free: face creams, trainers, track pants. If you're interested, you can get it all for a good price – my sister set up a shop on eBay.

And as for the acting, I just asked Anne May, the drama teacher at Notley High School. She was a lovely lady. Obviously, being an actor, she had a lot of gay friends and she sniffed me out straightaway. She decided the best part for me to play was Puck. I was like 'F***' I can't even speak modern-day English, let alone get all olde worlde with a bit of Shakespeare. But Puck it was, and Puck I did (I said Puck!).

> The king doth keep his revels here tonight,
> Take heed the Queen come not within his sight.
> For Oberon is passing fell and wroth
> Because that she, as her attendant hath
> A young boy stolen from an Indian king.

That's all I can remember and it may not be perfect, but that's how I did it.

So, I had 'Happy Birthday' for my song, Puck (F***) for my acting piece, and now to the bit that I could do. It was Lyrical Jazz, a beautiful dance style that I discovered (but obviously had been discovered long before me). This was a style I felt at one with, it was my trump card, my ace.

It was choreographed by Dadina and Doreen. Dadina gave me the Lyrical Jazz and Doreen inserted the acrobatics. This was my forte, and I had to blow them away if I was to get in. And on the day I almost did: I was so nervous, I couldn't stop farting. In Lycra, it's not a good look; it's that tight, you could see the bubble going down my leg.

I had moved on from the Lycra with the disco tassels. I was much more sophisticated and on trend with what was happening. It was a sleeveless black-vest top style, all-in-one cotton Lycra, three-quarter length, no stirrups. It was very big in the Eighties, cotton Lycra, as I'm sure all you girls (and some of you gays) will remember. I'm sure some of you had the popper stud or velcro leotards, with your leggings and mini to match. This time I did mail order and bypassed the shop in Braintree that only stocked women's wear. Dadina bought it for me from Freeds in London.

I was also treated to my first pork strap, or jockstrap, whatever you want to call it. It's quite a strange experience, really, putting it on for the first time. Let me explain it for you: a man's dance support strap isn't like a man's sport support strap. Sports straps have two pieces of elastic on the outside of each butt cheek, which give lift and support both sides.

When you train as a dancer, working your gluteus maximus (that's your ass, to anyone from Essex), you don't need the side support. It's straight up your back crack like a cheese

The Italia Conti Academy of Theatre Arts Ltd.

72 LANDOR ROAD LONDON SW9 9TH
TELEPHONE 01 733 1652

3.1.83

Dear Mr & Mrs Spence

Re: APPLICATION FOR FULL TIME COURSE.

Thank you for your audition application form.
We are pleased to inform you that we have arranged an audition for Louie at 12.30pm on 7th April 83.

Please ensure you bring copies of your acting pieces and that your music is clearly marked.

Please arrive 10 minutes before the stated audition time.

Yours faithfully,

G. Skewsel

for ITALIA CONTI ACADEMY OF THEATRE ARTS LTD.

wire. I can't remember if my balls had dropped or not by age 12, but it looked like I had a vagina. It really did its job, the Cotton Lycra jock strap, and held you in.

So, everything was in place, including my balls. All I had to do was get it right on the day. And that day was getting nearer. I had to wait two months after the letter arrived for my audition and those two months felt like two years. As you know, when you're that young, time never seems to pass. Unlike now – by the time this book comes out, which should be pretty soon, you might have forgotten about me. No, I don't think you will have forgotten me. How could you forget me?!

I HAD not slept for most of the night before the audition and it was the first time that had happened. Not even at Christmas had this occurred to me. I know I keep saying I can remember things clearly, but I am very alert: I was fearful, worried, anxious because I knew it was make or break and could really change my life; and I was making, I was not about to be broken.

I met Doreen at 7.30 am at Braintree Station (Dadina could not come because she was doing a professional dance job); we were on the commuter run and I had never seen so many men in suits. It was a bit of a fight for a seat really, but we did manage. I needed the rest; I might have been young, but I hadn't slept all night. My anxiety started to kick in shortly into the journey and I was beginning to feel nauseous. I think it had something to do with the cigarette smoke in the carriage, but I managed to get through the journey of one hour and 10 minutes, then a tube trip. I felt ill again on the tube, being pushed and squashed between all those grown-ups. It was not what I needed before facing the biggest day of my life.

We finally reached Clapham North and my nerves almost got the better of me. I had read the name Clapham North on

the audition letter so many times: 'On leaving Clapham North, bear to the right, and there you will see Landor Road'. I can't remember the number but I can clearly remember the sounds and smells of showbusiness. I could hear a piano being played in one studio, pop music coming from another, while some students sang in the stairwells. It was like the fabric of the building was alive.

It was not a glamorous building by any means; thinking back, it was actually quite run down. But at that time, to me it seemed like the brightest, shiniest, most welcoming door I had ever opened in my life. I had to get through the audition and I had to be accepted into the school – it was where I belonged.

My dreams of being a dancer like those I used to watch on the big variety shows on Saturday nights were closer to becoming reality. I used to sit in front of the TV and think to myself, 'I want to be one of those boys.' I was inspired by watching them dance; in Braintree I seemed to be the only boy attending dance classes. There were a couple of male dancers in particular that I used to see on all the variety shows, such as *Royal Variety Performance* and *The Marti Caine Show*.

One of them was Eurasian, with long, jet-black hair that swished as he danced. The other was blond, with blue eyes; I say he was blond, but really, he had highlights. If there was a female artist on the show, he seemed to be the one who always danced with or close to them.

Years later, when I was taking classes at Pineapple, a friend introduced me to him. I literally gasped when I met him. His name was Greg and I thought to myself, 'If he only knew how much I used to fancy him!'

After reporting to reception we were sent to a room with the other auditionees and that was when reality finally kicked in. I was not the only one hoping to get in and places were limited. It was not a comprehensive school and they could only accommodate so many students per year. One advantage in being a boy was that there were never as many of you fighting for a place. On my audition day there was one other boy and out of about 20 kids, I was one of the last to audition.

If it was just about dancing, it would have been easy for me. I could check out the competition auditioning in the studio next to the room we were waiting in and, worse for me, we could hear them singing – and the other boy was not singing 'Happy Birthday', nor was he singing out of tune. He was singing like an angel sent from heaven. That's when I had one of my very first gay moments, calling him a bitch. In my mind, of course, not out loud.

I questioned myself for a moment, wondering why I was calling him a bitch, but it was only a moment. But then I remembered: I was different, or special, as I like to call it in my own mind. Then it was my turn.

'Louie Spence, please.'

My heart was pumping so fast and I was shaking that much – when I went into the studio the first thing I saw was the panel that was going to judge me. They sat behind a long table and looked very stern. Each one had a notepad and a glass of water in front of them. There were two women and two men.

The first lady looked like a headmistress and was in fact the principal of the school. She seemed to be in her fifties. She was very well-groomed and wore a two-piece tweed suit. It was blue with yellow flecks and the jacket had three big gold buttons. Her hair was in a chignon and she wore oval tortoiseshell glasses.

Next to her was a younger man in his forties, with thick brown, greying hair that had a sharp side parting. His beard was unkempt and he wore a dowdy dark blazer that you would find on most history or geography teachers.

Next was a middle-aged lady with crazy dark-brown hair, with a soft frizzy perm. Throughout the audition she twisted her hair through her fingers, tousling and teasing it. She wore thick mascara, which gave her three large lashes on each eye. Her lipstick was bright red and could have stopped traffic. She wore an off-the-shoulder top, which she shifted off one shoulder to the other throughout the audition and I found this very off-putting.

To her left was the pianist. He wore stone-washed jeans and a leather biker jacket, which I thought was an odd choice. I found out later he did not have a motorbike and looking back, I can see it was a gay fashion and that he was a leather queen.

They asked my name and I had a vibrato in my voice. Unfortunately it did not help my rendition of 'Happy Birthday'. The panel was very to the point and told me my vocal performance needed a lot of work. In my mind again, I was thinking, 'Tell me something I don't know.'

Next was the piece from Shakespeare, which received pretty much the same response. At this point I could feel my dream slipping away from me – I knew this was it. I had to make it work. When I knew I had to dance everything became a blur and the panel seemed to speak in slow motion. I lost myself in the dance and when I finished, I could not remember starting, what was in the middle or getting to the end. What I could see was the panel applauding my performance and nodding in a way that reassured me that they understood who I was and what I was about.

I just had to hope that it would be enough because my singing and acting were definitely not up to scratch. I left the audition happy but very apprehensive, knowing that I would have to wait up to six weeks for their decision. I could not think about anything else for those two months and if you don't know what I mean, think back to your first love: when you couldn't sleep, you couldn't think, you couldn't eat. Dance was *my* first love and I didn't want it to end: I was going to be faithful and loving for ever and ever, and it is true. Still to this day, even if I have nothing else in my life, no-one can take my love of dance away from me because it truly is part of who I am.

5
A Big Wrench

As we all know, and we've all done at some point, we agree to things for love that we wouldn't normally even consider. I say 'agree': I actually offered my services for free at John's Tyres and Exhausts – yes, you have read it right. *Me* – working at a tyre depot.

I had decided to give up my Saturday morning dance classes to prove how much I wanted this; if my parents and family were prepared to make sacrifices, I knew I had to do the same. I would face this challenge full-on.

It was called John's Tyres and Exhausts because it was my dad's, John's – well there were a couple of partners, I don't really know, I was only a kid. When Dad accepted my offer, the enormity of what I had suggested to him hit me like a Louboutin over the head.

Shit!

You see, the thing is, I had never really spent much time with Dad. One, because he was always working and he just wasn't the kind of dad who would take us swimming or playing football. Not that I wanted to play football! I was more than happy in my Lycra, thank you very much. And it wasn't just with me, he was also like that with my sisters. It was just the kind of dad he was.

We never felt for a second unloved by him; he is, and was the kindest, funniest man you could wish to meet. Everyone seemed to fall in love with him because he could always crack a joke and make you smile. I suppose I get my sense of humour from him, but with a lot more camp.

The thought of having to spend a whole day with my dad – what was I going to talk about? At 12 I had already discovered masturbation and I knocked my first one out in the downstairs loo. But I didn't really want to discuss that with him, especially when it was about Mr Whippy!

At that point I couldn't have told you the difference between a remould tyre, a back box or whether your tracking needed doing. Not that I didn't find out! I'll give you my tyre and exhaust knowledge later on – I think you'll be surprised.

I suppose what I'm trying to say, at 41 years old, is that I love my dad.

Even at the age of 12 I knew I was gay, and I was very comfortable with who I was. My family didn't treat me any differently for being a high-kicking, backflipping, Lycra-wearing gay but there were certain situations when I felt uncomfortable with Dad. Now, I was never bullied – I *was* called poof, fairy, whatever, but it didn't bother me in the slightest. The only time it would have bothered me is when I would have been with Dad.

I know that he would have wanted to protect me and would have stood up for me in such a situation, and I didn't want him to be put in that situation because of me. Because it truly, truly did not bother me. I suppose that's why, if there were situations that arose when Dad asked me to do something with him, I would always say no, just in case somebody did make a comment about me and my lisp, or my knowledge of women's fashion and make-up. That's only because Mum used to sell Oriflame, which was a brand of make-up. And I wouldn't miss a Wednesday going down to the market with her, helping her choose a dress for a night out at the Windmill Club with the girls, in Copford, near Colchester.

So, how was I going to cope with a whole day down at the tyre depot, with mechanics in grease-stained overalls smelling of man sweat? Well, if you offered me the chance now, I'd be more than happy: I'd jump at it and fix a puncture.

Back then, I didn't know if I would be able to cope with being a tea-boy and having to work in a filthy kitchen. I say kitchen, it was a piece of MDF and some dirty mugs, next to the toilet – I'm sure it wouldn't pass Health and Safety these days. But I had offered my services for my love of dance and it had to be followed through, and so it was.

SATURDAY MORNING, 6.30 rise. Tea and toast with Dad. Now the day had only just started and already this felt awkward. We didn't have much to talk about over tea and toast, and I had a whole day to get through, not only with Dad but with all the other men who worked at the tyre

depot, one of them being Uncle Glen, who would constantly take the piss out of me.

I knew that none of them would be interested in the disco flip, or rib isolations; maybe a pelvic thrust would have been interesting. Women always tell me they like a man with a good pelvic thrust. But this wouldn't do. Football? Shit, I didn't have a clue. Page 3. There you go! That's what I would do, I would concentrate on Page 3.

There we were in the car, it was only a 10-minute drive. Still nothing to talk about: I didn't want to exhaust my Page 3 conversation with Dad, it had to get me through the morning with five of them.

Dad always arrived first because he would open up and as soon as the door was open, quicker than you could say 'gay', I had the marigolds on with my hands down the toilet, trying to scrub the brown-stained bowl. I just couldn't help it, even though I'd told myself, 'butch, butch, butch' – it was just instinctive. Well, it's not all my fault actually: I'm sorry, I was just following what Mum did. And yes, the mugs were being soaked in bleach and I'd nicked a bit of Shake'n'Vac from home, which I sprinkled on the carpet tiles on my way in.

Well, I was pleasantly surprised: all the boys were very happy to come in to a clean toilet, a fresh-smelling reception area with tiled surfaces shiny enough to reflect your face. They were more than happy to have someone with a feminine touch around them. And for me, I can look back on it as a really happy time bonding with my dad and not feeling uncomfortable with who I was around his work colleagues and friends. In fact, believe it or not, I really looked forward to Saturday mornings at the depot. I was promoted from tea-boy to puncture boy, but that didn't mean that I used to get punched all day. When customers brought their punctured tyres in, I would take the tyres from them, 'thank you very much, sir'. I would blow them up with the air gun and place it in the water butt, which was like a big paddling pool full of water. It was very dirty water: it didn't get changed every day, so I always had my marigolds in my overall pocket. Yes, I was also wearing a pair of blue, grease-stained overalls at this point.

Obviously I would always work a look with it. I would have the top rolled down with the arms wrapped around twice, with the bow featuring on the side. At that age, I had a 23-inch waist.

While the tyre was in the water butt you had to check to see where the bubbles were coming from to indicate escaping air. Then you would take a piece of yellow chalk from your pocket and mark the spot with an X. Don't ask me why it was yellow, but it was. You would then roll the tyre over to the breaking-down machine. I don't know if that is the correct name for it, but you would remove the tyre from the wheel rim and see if it was repairable.

If it was repairable, you would put a rubber patch on it (after putting glue on), and get a roller and roll over the patch until it was sealed, put the tyre back on the wheel rim and hopefully, Bob's your uncle, Fanny's your aunt and it's fixed. Now, if this didn't work, you had a second option: you could just stick an inner tube in because a lot of tyres were tubeless, you see. Are you following me, or have I lost you with my immense knowledge of puncture repair?

I'm not going to bore you with tracking, or holes in your back box (you could just fill it up with a bit of gum or weld it). It would be cheaper than buying a new exhaust.

Surprised? Yes, I thought you would be. I did have my moments. But this was all for a reason, and the reason had arrived.

CRASH, BANG, wallop, there it was! On the porch floor, my letter from Italia Conti. Oh, before I get to that – yes, we had a porch. Not only did we have a porch, we had patio doors at the back: we were fully double-glazed with a picture window at the front, brick wall at the front and a wrought-iron gate.

There weren't many houses like that on the Goldingham; this was part of the problem, you see. Pat and John, Mum and Dad, had bought their council house in 1978. Well, you can imagine Mum – as soon as she got a mortgage, not only did she have her tits done, which she thought we all didn't notice when she came back from her 'holiday' in Billericay. For some reason she couldn't lift her arms and she suddenly had tits. I mean, really, for someone who used to shop for all her dresses with her, I knew something had changed but I just went with it, I wasn't about to kick up a fuss.

The fact was that she looked truly amazing in her tube dresses: out at the front, in at the waist and out at the back. She really did turn heads, so those tits were worth every penny of the mortgage money. As were all the improvements that she made to the house – the only problem was all this money was spent before Italia Conti was even mentioned and my wage from John's Tyres and Exhaust wouldn't have even paid for the school cap.

Mum showing off her new boobs in one of her
backless dresses; no bra needed!

So, here was the moment that I had been waiting for after two months, there in front of me. I wanted to rip it open, but it was not addressed to me. On the other hand, I didn't want to know what was inside, in case it was not 'yes'. Dad had already gone to work, so it was down to Mum to open it and let me know my fate, but at the end of the day it was not my choice, it would be down to Mum and Dad.

I watched Mum's face intently as she opened the letter and started to read it. There was no expression, no sudden cry of 'You've got in! I can't believe it'. Nor were there tears for me, her expression remained blank. Finally, she told me that I had been accepted and at this point you think I would high kick, back flip and scream, but I didn't.

I could tell from Mum's face, even though it was a 'yes', there was a big chance/probability of me not going. Dad's business was not going so well and they had just taken out a huge mortgage on the house – and Mum had already spent the first term's fee on her tits.

As you can imagine, it was a bittersweet moment. It was all now dependent on Dad, as he was the main breadwinner. I knew I had proved to him how much I wanted this by giving up my dance classes on Saturdays to go and work with him at the tyre depot, but as he had made very clear to me, money did not grow on trees and times were hard. It might just not be possible to find another few thousand pounds each term, but Dad did the most incredible thing for me.

He put his house and business at risk by taking out a second mortgage to pay for my school fees for the next four years. It was at that moment that I understood that when you love someone unconditionally, you will do anything for them if you can. Although, as I said, Dad wasn't someone who took us to the park to play on the swings and all of those things, he would work every hour of the day to make sure all of his children were happy and were given the best opportunities in life. If it wasn't for him doing that for me, I would not have experienced and be living the most amazing life that I have.

Saying 'I love you' can sometimes be meaningless when they are only words, but what he has done for me no words can fully express: it is beyond love. Right, that's it, I can feel a tear welling up. Yes, you've all just witnessed me telling my dad how much I love him, which I don't do. But it's done: so, thanks for that, Dad! That's if he reads this! He's never read a book in his life. Maybe they'll serialise it in the *Sun* – that's as much as he'll read.

IF YOU haven't worked it out, I got in to Italia Conti and my life truly began.

There are so many things I can remember really clearly, but my first day at Italia Conti – I can't recall a bloody thing! I was so filled with nerves and excitement that it is all of a blur. Things were so different at Italia Conti compared to school. In the morning, we would do what was called 'school rooms': English, Maths, French, etc. In the afternoon, you would do your singing, your dancing, your acting. It was just amazing and I loved it.

I say I loved it; I didn't love it all. I still didn't like the academic side of it, but it was more interesting than at a normal comprehensive school. Everyone was theatrical, so there was always a drama going on somewhere in class. Someone had just got a part in *Grange Hill*, someone else didn't get the commercial they went for. You see, there was an agency at the school and casting agents would get in contact with the agency and tell them exactly what they were looking for. Whenever you came out of class, you would always check to see if your name was up on the board, calling you to a casting at the agency.

It was amazing. One of my first jobs was as an extra on *Grange Hill* – it was so surreal. To think one minute I was watching it, and the next I was on the set. Camera, lights, action! Everyone at stage school seemed so much more grown-up – talking about work, and how much they were earning for this, how much they got paid for that. Some of those kids were earning a lot of money at 13 or 14, especially the regular parts. We had a few regulars in *Grange Hill* at Italia Conti. Don't ask me what the character names were.

Naomi Campbell was in the year below me at Italia Conti; when she did her campaign for Hyper Hyper, a popular clothing store, her face was everywhere. Kids would say, 'Have you seen Naomi?' You couldn't miss her, she was all over every tube station. She didn't do too badly, did she? I find it really funny when I read stories about her – I remember her as a shy, timid, lovely girl. She was only 14. We all change, don't we?

Another job I got when I was at Conti's was on the *Hot Shoe Show*, which was a massive dance show on TV, on Saturday or Sunday night. It starred Wayne Sleep and Bonnie Langford and Cherry Gillespie, who was in Pan's People or Hot Gossip, or both, I can't remember. Anyway, it was an amazing show. Arlene Phillips was a choreographer on the show, although she didn't choreograph my number. I did a tap dance along with about eight other boys and Wayne Sleep. There was a height requirement on the job, none of us could be taller than Wayne, so we must all have been around five foot two at that time.

And you know who else did it with me? John Partridge from *EastEnders* – he plays the gay character, Christian. You see, we've all been at it a long time. We rehearsed for about a week and I can remember the professionals, like Bonnie, rehearsing in the studio next door. I would think, that's what I want to do, I want to dance like that. They were doing all the things I wanted to do, but with a lot more precision, obviously. Beautiful, lyrical combinations, high-kicking and pirouetting (pirouettes are when you see dancers turn on one leg), and making it look all so easy.

I never would have thought then that a few years later (quite a few years later) I would have been in class with these dancers at Pineapple, dancing alongside them and may I add, giving them a run for their money.

And then there was the biggest job I did as a child – biggest job because it was a West End show. When you are a child, you can only work a certain number of days per year. I think it was about three months.

I was called to the agency to go for an audition for *Bugsy Malone* the musical. Obviously, I had seen the film – what theatrical child would not want to be in a show like *Bugsy Malone*? You can imagine, every boy in school wanted to go up for it, but only about 10 of us got chosen to audition. We were told that you had to be able to tap-dance well, which was fine, thanks to Doreen Cliff. Even though Italia Conti was amazing, their classical ballet was not up to much. But, thank goodness, their tap classes were amazing. We had a lovely tap teacher named Ms Swivel. She was really quite strict, but she guaranteed we never missed a beat. So that box was ticked, but that was true for every other boy who was chosen to audition because of the high standard of tap teaching at the school. But then came my trump card! They wanted to know if anyone could do acrobatics!

Now, as well as being trampoline champion, I was also a pretty mean tumbler, thanks to the local farmers. When they cut the hay in the fields, we would do backflips and summersaults on the hay stacks. Being a natural, I graduated from hay to grass, and from grass to concrete – I had no fear.

I knew this job could be mine and then we were narrowed down to four boys. We were all similar tap dancers, so it was down to our tricks to separate us. Breakdancing was very big at the time, but it wasn't what they were looking for in a 1930s musical, so now it was down to three.

I mean, really, a hand spring? I was doing that aged three. So, now it's down to two.

A one-handed cartwheel? Really? I knew the job was mine, but I hadn't quite finished yet. I wasn't just going to get this job, I was going to get it with flying colours.

When they said to me, 'And what can you do, Louie?' I could feel my heart pumping with adrenaline. I took myself to the corner of the rehearsal room, where I proceeded to do Arab spring, five backflips, open-layout summersault, landing in splits. There are some jobs you just know you have won and at this point, with the panel on their feet applauding and the other boys looking very dejected, I realised this was one of those jobs.

Mum and Dad were pleased and relieved when I started to earn money from dancing. They used to give me 10 pounds every now and then, and did whatever they could on top of paying for my fees. This job was a great support and help for them, as the money I earned helped to pay for things I would need at Italia Conti, such as uniforms, which were very expensive, and my dance clothes.

And what a job it was. We rehearsed at Pineapple Studios and at the theatre, Her Majesty's, in Haymarket. We also got to stay in a hotel for three months, which was great fun, sharing with two other boys in the show.

I remember one evening looking out of the window to the hotel opposite and I saw a couple having sex. He was a lot older than her and even at that age, we figured out that she must have been a prostitute. For some reason he was wearing a 10-gallon hat. By the time they finished, we had the entire cast of *Bugsy Malone* watching. When our chaperone on the show realised what we were watching, she nearly had a cardiac, bless her! She was a sweet little Irish lady, but she never really looked after us. As soon as we got back to the hotel she went straight to her room, feet up. Not that we needed looking after – showbiz kids are always older than their age. In fact, I think we used to look after her.

The first night of the show was amazing. I had a coach trip come up from Braintree – sisters, aunties, friends – to support me. When I met Mum and Dad after the show, I could see how proud they were. I think it was at that point when they realised they had done the right thing in sending me to Italia Conti.

I certainly knew it was the right thing: everything about the place just felt so right. Everyone was so much older in the

way they conducted themselves, so aware of who they were and also what they wanted. We all knew we wanted a career in showbusiness, whether it was as a dancer, actor or singer. Everyone had an incredible creative energy, the whole place felt as though it was buzzing. Even though I used to dread getting up in the morning at 5.30, especially in the winter when it was cold and dark outside, when no-one else was awake in the house, just me creeping around having a cup of tea and marmite on toast, before a 20-minute walk to the station, before an hour and 40-minute train ride to school. That's if there wasn't snow, or leaves on the track – but whatever, it was so worth it.

As soon as I walked through the school doors it was showtime – every day was a performance. Someone was always working towards something, for an audition or a film, or just practising what they had done the day before. I can't remember any negativity – everyone was encouraging and if you were down, you could guarantee in five minutes you would be laughing – there were so many wonderful characters. See, I am one of those people who is not very good with names but I never forget a face, but the group of people I can remember included a girl called Janine, who used to sit next to me in class. We were as bad as each other: we hated academic work and would sit laughing in class before being kicked out, when we would laugh even more.

Then there was Vanessa, whose sister also attended Italia Conti – I don't know how her parents did it. And then there was Tina Foley – her first and last name seemed to go together, so I remember hers. She had really big boobs as well.

STILL GOT IT, NEVER LOST IT!

This is to certify

LOUIE SPENCE

appeared in

Bugsy Malone

at

Her Majesty's Theatre
Haymarket
London SW1

From 22ND DEC 1983 to 11TH FEBRUARY 1984.

_____
Martin Gates
Producer/Director

_____
Gillian Gregory
Choreographer

_____
Philip Summerscales
Producer

_____
Sue Radley
Casting Director

_____
Lars Sternmarker
Associate Producer

69

Gary had a Sta-Sof-Fro hairdo, which used to drip on to his collar jacket. Absolutely beautiful, and would give Naomi a run – now he's Sade, and I mean completely Sade. The complete lot gone, the *big chop* – he makes a stunning lady.

ONE DAY we bunked off school – me, Gary and John (who I'll tell you about later) – and went to Julia Sawalha's house – you may know her as Saffy, the long-suffering daughter in *Absolutely Fabulous* and one of the stars of *Lark Rise to Candleford*. We got the tube to Brixton, which was my first time there. All I had ever heard of it was the riots, so I expected a war zone but it was nothing like that at all. It was quite nice – we had a walk around Morleys, which was like a really cheap version of Selfridges, and bought a few provisions for our day of bunking off. Then we were met by one of Julia's older sisters (Nadia or possibly Dina; if she wasn't Nadia, she looked like her). She was beautiful, with long brown-blonde hair and lovely skin.

Julia was the same, she was very beautiful. She had lovely feet as well – I haven't got a foot fetish, I mean lovely for dancing. She had a naturally beautiful arch, or instep. So even though we were bunking off, it was very well-arranged. Her parents were away and her sister came to pick us up – we went to visit her in South Norwood, I think. The house was lovely, big and looked expensive. We had a very nice council house with all the trimmings, but this house was something else. Their furniture wasn't from MFI and there wasn't a bit of Artex or wood panelling inside.

When Artex came out, our house was done top to bottom, swirl and dry. The only problem was if you walked past and fell into it, you'd be stabbed by the prickly bits that stuck out, where Dad had got a really good pull on the swirl. I'd wake up some mornings and look as if I'd been dragged backwards through a hedge.

No, all the furniture in their house was solid and real. The dining-room table was proper wood – you could see it had been a tree. It was not for convenience and it didn't have an easy-wipe surface: the table would definitely have needed a French polish.

Even though it would really piss my parents off to know that I was bunking off after all the sacrifices they had made, it was the first time I had done it. It didn't feel like I was bunking off because it was all so well-arranged, but I am so glad I did. It wasn't like we were hiding up in the farmer's fields, or in some dirty garage, with a mouldy old sofa and a wet mattress. Because that was how they used to bunk off in Braintree, in my dad's old garage that he never used, all sitting around on that smelly sofa smoking their Rothman Royals. No, not me, I was doing the VIP bunking off.

Julia's sister was cooking us lunch while we popped off down to the video shop to get ourselves a couple of films for the day. I'm sure we must have got something like *The Sound of Music* or *Annie*. But I remember perfectly the third video we got. It was included free with the other two and was called *I Want to Be a Woman*. I can't remember who chose it, but it wasn't me; it must have been on the top shelf and there's no way I could have reached that. (I only reached up to the Disney films at five foot two and a bit; looking back now, I think it might have been Gary/Sade.)

I Want to Be a Woman was a very detailed, step-by-step docufilm about a man who wanted to become a woman. Now I know you can now see that kind of thing on Channel 4 after the watershed, but it wasn't the kind of thing you saw on the telly back then. (In fact, as this was around 1982, Channel 4 had only just started.) All I can say is, I couldn't bear to eat a banana for years after – I couldn't peel the skin, because that's exactly what it was like. They just took the inside of the banana out, and wham, bam, alacazam, you are no longer a man!

But the end-product was amazing: it was very neat and tidy. I think transsexuals had the first designer vaginas. See, once again, we always lead the way in everything. And after that, I remember having my first moussaka. I wasn't sure if I was going to like it, because I hadn't been introduced to foreign food.

I poked at it for a bit, then said to John, who was sitting beside me, 'What's this purple thing?'

He replied, 'I think it's beetroot.'

Now, that was a surprise to me – I had only ever had beetroot in a salad. I didn't know that you could cook it in an oven. Of course, it was not beetroot. I know now that it was aubergine.

I could not see any meat in the dish and although it did not have potatoes on the top, I thought it might be a posh shepherd's pie.

Coming from a traditional-ish British family, fish wasn't fish to me if it didn't have breadcrumbs on it. The nearest we got to foreign food was pasta, which wasn't really pasta but spaghetti hoops – well, it had spaghetti in the title, didn't it? I later found out that spaghetti came with many things, but the one thing it didn't come in was a tin: it was normally in a packet that you put in water with a bit of salt.

I said to Julia, 'Is there meat in this?'

She said, 'No, it's vegetarian.'

I didn't have a clue what she meant. Vegetarian? She might as well have said 'homosexual', as if I knew. You don't get many of those in Braintree, vegetarians that is.

There was a water jug on the table, which surprised me. Why would you have water on the table when you could get it out of the tap? There was never room on our table at home for water, alongside the ketchup and brown sauce, and the salt and vinegar.

One of the chairs alone in Julia's kitchen would have filled our kitchen back in Braintree. They were large and made out of real wood. I thought everything looked real, none of it was fake. It was like seeing the actual furniture that ours at home was copied from. I didn't know that tables could have wooden legs – I thought they all had metal legs. And I was frightened that I was going to mark a piece of the furniture, but it all seemed so natural to Julia.

See, this is my point: bunking off school isn't always a negative thing. I learned a lot that day. For one, I learned even though I may have been camper than the average kid on the block, I quite liked my banana as it was. And, two, just because something has a foreign name like moussaka, it doesn't mean you shouldn't give it a go, because I did – and I loved it.

And I also learned a new word that day: couscous. Because I could, and because I can, because I did! It was also, on that day, I planned – along with John – another first. I say planned, but it was John, because he had already done it. Oh, what? I hear you ask, 'Oh what, oh what, oh *what*?'

Going to my first gay club. We were going to Heaven.

Now, I know this seems wrong, whether you're gay or straight, it's wrong. John had an older boyfriend: John was 14 and as I said, a lot of the kids at school were older than their years. He looked very mature for his age, he looked about 18 and had facial hair, so his boyfriend believed him when he lied about his age. He had told the boyfriend that he was over 18. The boyfriend was about 21, and when you're 14 it just seemed glamorous, and he used to come into school and tell us where he'd been, where they had been to dinner, which clubs they had gone to.

The last thing I wanted was a boyfriend. I wasn't interested at all – in fact, it frightened the life out of me but I was intrigued by this place that John described, where there were hundreds of gay men of all different shapes, sizes and colours. Butch ones, camp ones, drag queens – I couldn't wait to see this!

This is another thing that would have given Mum a nervous breakdown if she had known. Luckily she didn't, and when she reads this book, it will be the first time she knows. So, it was set, it was planned, we were doing it.

It was a Wednesday night, and the night was called Pyramid – at Heaven, under the arches at Charing Cross – and it was a student night. John used to speak about it all the

time. As I said, he looked older than his years but I would only have got in on a student night; I didn't have any facial hair, but I had spiky long hair. I suppose I could have passed as a pretty young lesbian.

Anyway, the day had come: school had finished and we got on the bus to Poplar, to John's house. We were accompanied by Lisa York, who had a lead part in *Grange Hill*. I remember thinking how cool she was, and all the kids knew who she was. John lived with his sister, I think their parents had died. His sister was quite liberal with him – he could go out at night, see his friends, and do what he wanted.

When we reached his house and in earshot of his sister, I asked what time we were going to Heaven. It became clear that his sister might have been liberal, but she wasn't so liberal that she would let her 14-year-old brother go to a gay club with his lesbian-looking friend – the way John looked at me, mouthing 'shut up'. I had nearly ruined my chances of going to Heaven. Shit, that would have been a nightmare because it was such a fabulous evening.

I spent the whole time on the bus there panicking, thinking I would be turned away at the door. I didn't care about getting turned away from the Alec Hunter school disco in Braintree – I mean, really! Most of the kids were outside having a fag. Or they were behind the science labs playing with each other and neither of those things appealed to me. Smoking gives you bad breath, but I did try it once with a girl down the ditch after I had eaten my Fab lolly with the hundreds and thousands on it. I had a poke around with my lollipop stick, but it was not for me.

So we got off the bus at Trafalgar Square and walked down to Charing Cross – and I couldn't believe it. There was a queue going right around the corner. Even though at 14 you could be naive, I knew this was where we were going. The queue was full of gay men – I guess you could say this was the first time my gaydar kicked in. I remember thinking, once we got in the queue, that everyone was looking at me and knew that I wasn't old enough to be there. The closer we got to the door, the more anxious and scared I was becoming. I was shaking on the inside and I could feel myself starting to shake on the outside. When there were only a few people in front of me, I could have passed out: I felt so scared, but very excited and nervous too.

I could see people being turned away by the bouncers on the door; I was too far away to hear what they were being asked, or why they were being turned away. I thought I wouldn't be able to speak, nothing would come out. But for some reason, don't ask me why, when it was our turn to walk past the bouncers, not a question was asked. We just slipped in like butter; I do think they assumed I was just a pretty young lesbian. But pretty lesbian or not, I was in.

The first thing that hit me was that nightclub smell: cigarette smoke engrained in the carpet, the air a little bit damp and moist, but most of all, the smell of alcohol. It reminded me of when I used to go to the under-16 discos at the local nightclubs, that same smell. But it was very unlike those under-16 nights: once we'd made our way down the 20 or so steps that lead down into Heaven and turned the corner, there it was – Gay Heaven! Maybe that's why they called the club Heaven, because whenever anyone walked down the stairs and turned the corner, they thought they were in Gay Heaven.

I had excited butterflies in my belly: I couldn't take

everything in, it was too much. Everything John had said was true, there really was every kind of gay man – black, white, blond, Chinese, thin, fat, short, tall. Where does a 14-year-old start? Now, I never really had a type but I suppose this was the first time I started to look more closely and pick up on things that attracted me. But it was so difficult because there were so many men, so little time. I'm sorry, I just couldn't resist saying that, but it's true.

I mean, I had never seen a gay black man, or a gay Chinese man, so this was something that attracted me because I had never seen it, just the stereotypical ones in magazines. I couldn't work out if this attracted me because I liked it, or because I had never seen it. And then there were boys who looked like those on the estate where I grew up. Then I saw the most gorgeous, dark-haired, dark-eyed, Latino-looking boy, who looked about 16 or 17.

That was when I first discovered my type. I could feel my jaw dropping as this vision in ripped jeans walked past; I couldn't take my eyes off him and everything seemed to slow down around me. I was momentarily and officially in love as I watched him walk the length of the club. Of course he didn't even see me, but I bet if I was to look at him now, he would turn his head.

John met up with his boyfriend in the club after we arrived and he was busy being 18, leaving me to fall in love and explore the club on my own. There were three levels – the ground floor, a smaller, more intimate bar area on the second level; there were lots of couples there, sitting on sofas, kissing. I must have looked like an idiot, staring; I had never seen so many men show affection to each other in this way. Even though I knew that this was who I was, I still felt a little bit uncomfortable seeing it in public.

On the third level everyone was letting rip in a disco-dancing frenzy and as you can imagine, I may not have had my Lycra and my tassels, but I couldn't resist getting on that dance floor and knocking out my disco thrust.

This was amazing; everyone in the club was so happy and alive. No-one looked at you in a critical manner: there didn't seem to be any prejudice, and I can truly say it was one of the best experiences of my life. From that evening, I definitely knew I was not on my own and there were a lot more than just the few gays at school. There was a whole world of us and from what I had seen, we certainly knew how to live.

The rest of my evening was spent disco dancing on the third floor and hiding behind pillars spying on my Latino lover. May I add that even though John and I went to Heaven fairly regularly on a Wednesday night after that, I never saw the Latino again, but I have never lost sight of him in my mind.

When we left, I came out of the club a different person, happy and proud of who I was. It confirmed to me that it doesn't matter what other people think: it's about what makes you feel happy and what makes you feel good. Being me and never having to live a lie made me the happiest 14-year-old on the planet, as did every other day that followed while I was at Conti's: you were guaranteed to learn something new every day, in life lessons more than academic ones.

I LEFT Conti's unfortunately – I say unfortunately, it didn't bother me then and it doesn't bother me now – with no exams. It's all my fault for not being interested in the lessons. Well, it's not all my fault – some of the teachers were so uninspiring. I was put in for an O-Level in Art, but in the last term I had an argument with the teacher, so I didn't even do that.

So there I am at 16 after four wonderful years at Conti's. I would love to have stayed on into the Students (sixth form), but there was no way that was going to happen. There was no money left and I now had to get out there and prove my worth, which ended up being much more difficult than I thought.

The next year of my life was not so joyous as the previous four: it was grim and depressing. I knew it wasn't going to be easy, coming straight out of school and getting a job in performing arts but I felt fairly confident, having already worked as a child performer, about my dancing skills, which had helped me to stand out at school. Boy, was I about to get a shock.

I started by buying the *Stage* newspaper every week: I went through the auditions section (which had lots of jobs), but I was either too young or didn't have an Equity card. For those of you who don't know, Equity is an actors' and dancers' union, and in those days, to get your Equity card you had to work a certain amount of time in professional jobs. You could get this by doing summer season, panto-mimes, etc.

Remembering I had been such a hit at Butlin's in my youth, I thought they would be my first port of call – they were bound to remember me. Well, did they? Did they Puck! I sent off the application form with a passport-sized photo, including all my previous work. I thought this would give me an advantage over others, but here it was once again. The reply was, thank you for your application but unfortunately we do not employ anyone under the age of 18.

So, then I was in a real Catch-22 – to work, I needed my Equity card and to get my Equity card, I needed to work. The work that could get me an Equity contract didn't want to employ me because I was too young. What's a gay to do, stuck in Braintree? I couldn't believe where I was. It felt like the last four years had been a dream and that they hadn't really happened. I felt alone and uninspired, with nothing around me to stimulate my artistic needs. Am I sounding dramatic? But wait, there's a lot more drama to come.

After about six months of being at home, getting more and more depressed, I hated every member of my family, especially Mum. Not that she had done anything, but as we all know, it's so easy to be vile to the people you love the most. The only words I would grunt if I was asked anything, were 'I don't know', 'I don't care' and 'I hate you'. On top of this, those slight feelings of anxiety that I used to get were no longer slight: the anxiety was turning into fear and panic.

7

Panic

The panic attacks I had when I was younger paled in comparison to what was happening to me back at home in Braintree. I thought I would be stuck in Braintree, all my hopes and dreams fading; the more I thought about this, the worse my anxiety became.

Anyone who has ever had an anxiety attack will understand; those who haven't will find it hard to imagine. I will try to explain how it made me feel. These attacks would come from nowhere: I would be feeling absolutely fine in an environment in which I felt safe and secure, and for me it would start when I felt slightly light-headed. Then I would have a feeling of being outside my own body; everything would start to go light and I would feel as if I was floating slightly. I would then get a dry mouth and could feel my fingers and toes tingling. After this I would break out into a cold sweat and could feel the blood draining from my body. My heart would start to race; this was the panic really kicking in, and then I would feel as if I were going to white out.

Even though I never passed out, when this happened to me, for some reason I would go and look in the mirror, and this time not for vanity. It was to convince myself that this was happening, that I wasn't going mad. When I looked in the mirror, I could see the colour physically drain from my face. So the cycle would continue; never knowing when or where this was going to happen. I started to become anxious in every situation, losing the confidence and spirit that had been a part of me before.

These attacks were not a strange occurrence in my family. I don't care what anyone says – I think it is genetic. My dad and sister Kelly do not have them, but Mum and my two other sisters do. This made the whole situation worse for me: being in an environment where we were all constantly fighting these attacks was truly driving me mad.

Even writing about it can bring back certain feelings of anxiety. These panic attacks have been ongoing throughout my adult life although I'm much more in control of them now. I know that I'm not actually going to die from them: the worst that will happen is that I might pass out, but it is still something I beat myself up about. There are certain things that I cannot do because of the attacks, such as flying – unless I really have to. I have missed out on some truly amazing opportunities, not just through work but also with my partner – I could not physically put myself in a situation where I might have an attack.

I suppose the most awful thing about all this is not just my fears and phobias, but also my hypochondria, which is a by-product of the panic attacks. And I don't just worry about myself: you can never just have a headache, it must be a migraine. Toothache must mean an abscess, a temperature can only mean malaria. You can imagine what I am like with myself: a headache is automatically a brain tumour, to the point of going for brain scans; a stomach ache is bowel cancer. Achy legs mean DVT, and so on, and so on. I have had these attacks for so long now, my attitude is that we all have to live with things we don't like, and this is mine.

I can hear you all asking, 'Have you tried this, have you tried that?' Yes, yes, yes! I have tried more than this and that. I have had psychotherapy, acupuncture, every herbal remedy, Chinese medicine, hypnosis. I have read all the self-help books. (I say read them all, I'm lying really – I just got half-way through. Well, that's a lie too, I got a panic attack half-way through. So, no, they didn't work.) The only thing I haven't tried is any kind of prescription drug. I've seen some of the results that this kind of medication has. Yes, it can help to eradicate or relieve these symptoms and attacks in a big way but it can also make people detached and emotionless.

If I had a wish it would be for what I would call a normal life without all of these phobias, fears and distractions. However, medication is not the way for me. One thing I know about myself is that I live by my emotions and that is what makes me who I am.

I had a long period when these attacks felt as if they had almost gone. It was when I first started to work at Pineapple. I had never had a permanent job before, one that paid a regular wage. At the same time that I started to work at Pineapple, I met my husband. For 10 years, the attacks were very few and far between.

Just recently, believe it or not, they have become more frequent. This makes sense, as I would not be writing this book if my life had not changed quite dramatically. When you are someone who suffers with these attacks, situations like big crowds and enclosed spaces can trigger an attack. Now part of work involves being in big crowds, which can become closed in. So, if one of you ever sees me in one of those situations and I start looking a bit pasty and begin to white out, don't worry: I'm just having a panic attack.

I often think, 'Why me? What have I done to deserve this?' But I also believe you have to take the rough with the smooth and the good with the bad. Although these attacks continue to be a part of my life, if there is a God up there the flipside is that I have been blessed with the most incredible and fulfilled life I could ever have wished for. At 41, it is becoming more spectacular and more enriched than I could ever have imagined.

SO, BACK to the age of 16 when these attacks started to kick in. After I had been back at home for six months, Mum said those sacrilegious words, 'Well, you could always try and get a normal job, like everyone else,' even though she, I and everyone in Braintree knew there was nothing run-of-the-mill about me. I may have been a bit reclusive over the last six months, and not backflipping and high-kicking down the town centre, but my internal disco ball was still turning and shimmering deep within me. Mum's suggestion, of going to work down the local light factory, was enough to spin my disco ball into a gay frenzy.

How could I do this to myself? To work with these people, with no education, who most probably couldn't read or spell.

And then the reality kicked in: I actually couldn't spell and I did have to go into special needs class for my reading. I'm not ashamed; I didn't pass any GCSEs or O-Levels, not even a City & Guild's. Was I really me? Who was this person who was filling in an application form to work at the local light factory?

I told myself maybe that was where I did belong; with my lack of academic education, I would fit in well. Being able to high-kick and backflip made me no better than anyone else there. Well, lo and behold, I got the job! I suppose I did get to wear a red coat. I say coat, it was an overall. It didn't have the B for Butlin's, but it did have LE for Light Electronics.

I can honestly say, give me a panic attack any day. I may as well have been dead. Putting screws in light fittings – is this what I had become? From starring in the West End at 14 in *Bugsy Malone*, disco dancing on the third floor at Heaven, to this?

Oh no, this had certainly Whammed me – I woke up before I was going to gogo! I screwed my last light-fitting, I had made my mind up: if I was too young to get a job and couldn't get my Equity card, then I was going back to where I belonged. I was going to dance college – I wasn't about to die a slow, uneducated death.

The next application I would be filling in was for London Studio Centre. By this time, my parents had done everything they could for me and they were relieved.

I told Mum about my decision first and she agreed with it.

'I'm glad, Louie! We're sick of seeing you moping around here, as if the world has done you an injustice. You don't belong here, this town is not big enough for you. You need to be in London, where you belong.'

I was glad to hear her reaction: I realised I had been foul to my family for the last six months and now I had made the decision to move back to London, I was relieved when they agreed it was the best thing. I knew that I could not rely on my parents for any more assistance and the only way I was going to attend London Studio Centre was if I auditioned for a scholarship.

Luckily my audition was successful and I received a full scholarship.

Hallelujah! Can you all see the light shining? Because I saw it. I suppose there is a great lesson to be learned here. By doing something you really hate, and that makes you feel worthless, wearing a bad-fitting overall, makes you realise your true destiny and no matter what you have to do to get there, never give up on your dreams.

My life beginneth againeth!

8
London Studio Centre

Now London Studio Centre was a whole different ball game. I certainly knew who I was and what I wanted out of the next three years of my life: I wanted to become the best dancer I could be and nothing was going to stop me. Not even the fact that I had to slip on a tabard, working at the pick'n'mix at the Trocadero in Piccadilly to pay my rent for the flat I shared with three Italians on the Edgware Road. This is when I discovered a love for all things Italian, including pasta.

Thank God I didn't pick up all the things beloved by these Italians. Unknown to me, two of them were cocaine dealers. I found out when I moved out and took my suitcase. When I arrived at my new flat in Enfield and unpacked, there were lots of pieces of paper in the zip section of my case. They were all wrapped very nicely, but I couldn't work out what they were until I opened them and found a lot of white powder inside.

I had seen *Scarface* – I knew exactly what the powder was. When I saw the powder, my heart fell out of my ass:

one, because I had 10 of these envelopes; two, I had just crossed London in possession of these drugs and three, would Al Pacino be looking for me? Joking aside, I truly did shit myself. It was only a room I had in the flat with the Italians – they didn't know where I went to college, they didn't even know what I did. I wasn't about to traipse across London with 10 wraps in my bum bags. Do you remember bum bags? Anyway, I put them straight down the toilet and never told a soul, until now.

Well, I lie – I did tell one other person and that was my best friend, Carmine (who shared the new flat in Enfield with me). A lot of you may know him as Jake Canuso, or Matteo, the greasy waiter in *Benidorm*. Neither of us ever spoke a word of it. We were convinced we would be put in prison if anyone found out and if that happened, we wouldn't be able to get our free flyers to go out disco dancing every night.

The last thing I wanted was to be to be banged up in prison. I don't know how George Michael did it: I know people make jokes about it being a gay man's dream – I make them myself – but with my history of panic attacks, I don't think it would be fun for anyone. I'm bad in enclosed spaces and crowds as you know.

THINGS WERE going good for me: I was at a great college and living an independent life with my best friend, and still working at the pick'n'mix at the Trocadero. I also did a stint front of house at the Albery Theatre in St Martin's Lane, which turned out to be a very small stint. I got the sack for nicking the After Eights. I didn't nick the whole box, I only undid the seal from one side of the box, pushed the After Eights out, took out four or five or maybe 10, stuck the box back down and sold them on to the customers. The fact was, I should never have been facing the customers from that side of the curtain and I never did again: the next time I was in a theatre, I was on the stage.

London Studio Centre was so different to Conti's: this was not a place to discover yourself, it was a place of learning. The goal was to reach your true potential and I couldn't get enough of it. Each day could not come quickly enough – I was like a vampire starved of blood, I just had to dance.

I could feel myself getting stronger, not only because my body was starting to change but I was learning the art of technique. It doesn't matter what you do, whether you bake cakes or it's banging out babies, it's all to do with technique. I was very fortunate to have a teacher who spotted my potential; her name was Theresa Kerr. She used to teach a class called Rock Jazz, which was a combination of classical ballet and jazz dancing. When I say Jazz, that isn't dancing to jazz music – it's to any kind of music, but it lends itself to lyrical tracks. Whitney and Barbra (Streisand, that is) were always favourites for me – I love knocking out a routine to them.

The classes were normally 90 minutes long and sometimes the warm-up alone could be an hour and 15 minutes. You see, what was important to Theresa was that magic word, technique. In saying that, the warm-up was a dance in itself. What I learned from Theresa was that every movement is a dance. So, something that I viewed previously as a fairly mundane warm-up step was now shown to me in a different light – this is what made me so hungry. The steps were never-ending; this meant that I could never stop learning. That is still the case – I can still learn something new every day in dance.

This is what I wanted to do every day, and it is what I did. Fortunately for me, not only did Theresa teach twice a week – on Tuesdays and Thursdays, at London Studio Centre – she also had her own dance school in Cambridge, called Bodyworks, which became a huge part of my life during the three years I trained with her.

School holidays no longer existed for me, but this was from choice. I would move in with Theresa and her family during each holiday from school – Patrick, her husband, her daughters Jane, Emma and Lucy, and her son Tara. It was a real showbiz family. Patrick was also a dancer and taught tap at their school. The girls were all dancers and Tara, although he didn't dance, just went along with everything.

I used to dance at least six hours a day when I was in Cambridge, doing classes back to back. It was amazing. Certain things that seemed so far away that I would never be able to achieve them got closer and closer as each day went by. I would start off with one pirouette then two pirouettes. By the time I had finished with Theresa, I could quite comfortably do eight pirouettes on both sides, which means left and right in dancer terminology. On a good day, I could do 10 to the left. Most people turn to the right, but I am a left-turner – I guess I'm just a bit different to the rest.

It may be some people's nightmare, to talk shop or chat about work all the time, but this is what we did. We danced all day, then went home and watched dance. It was so Liquid Gold – we danced ourselves dizzy. (Those of you old enough will remember this was a disco song from 1980. The rest of you can Google it.)

With my intense training, this time I left college with a diploma: with Honours, in fact. I was also awarded Best Jazz Dancer in the college. Then I felt ready to go out into the big wide world of dance to let them know I had arrived. I thought things were going to be easy because of all the hard work I had put into my dance training, but as always in the dance industry, nothing came easy. It was OK being one of the best dancers in college, but that wasn't the real world.

The real world was the one I was now facing, having to make dance my profession as an adult, no longer able to depend on anyone but myself. The first thing I had to do was find myself an agent and get a Z-card. This is the card that has a couple of photos of you in different looks and poses, with your height and measurements. But it was not an easy task to get an agent straight out of college. Most good agents' books were full of working dancers and the only real way to get in was on a recommendation. As you can imagine, this didn't happen often: if you were better than the person who recommended you, you might end up getting their job.

This was not the right time to fall in love, but fall I did. But this time it wasn't with dance: it was the first romantic love I had experienced.

9
Piero

Now, you remember that tall, dark, handsome Latino that I saw in Heaven when I was 14? Well, Piero was a tall, dark, handsome Latino whom I met in Heaven one Saturday night when I was out with my best friend Carmine.

We had moved from Enfield to Finsbury Park, to a two-bedroom flat, and Carmine and I shared a room (as you do when you are young and unemployed, saving on the rent). We shared the flat with Ivan, a Swiss-French hairdresser. And every other Saturday, we would go into town, around Soho and the West End. It wasn't like it is now – there was only Compton's pub on Old Compton Street. For those of you who don't know Old Compton Street, if you come to London, take a mince down there: it's bright and colourful and full of gay men.

Anyway, we would come into town and go into Compton's, or Brief Encounter, which was another bar on St Martin's Lane, which is now the St Martin's Hotel. We went there to pick up flyers so we could get into Heaven for free before 11pm. Once we had our flyers, we would go shopping with money we didn't have – just put it on our overdrafts that we then couldn't afford to pay off, because none of those bloody dancers would give us a break and introduce us to an agent. But that wasn't going to stop us from living our lives to the full, in and out of every shop you could think of, trying on everything you could imagine.

But it was the Eighties, and I normally ended up going out in a leotard or a crop-top. No, not a leotard on its own – I would have a pair of nicely ripped jeans. Remember that inconspicuous rip just below your ass cheek that you would spend hours fraying to make it look as though it was always there?

After we had minced around the West End – and when I say minced, honestly, we could have put a butcher out of business. Then the whole process would start: from the minute we got back home, the music went on and we would start to get ready.

We had to be at Heaven before 11 pm and we would start at 5 pm, giving us roughly six hours to get ready and get to the club. There was never a minute to spare – we would start off with clothes, laying them out on the bed. I never had to iron my clothes. As I said, I usually wore a leotard and crop-top, the cotton Lycra saved precious time. And I needed all the time I could get: I was modelling a bob, one of those shaved underneath so if I pulled it back into a ponytail, I looked like a Samurai.

I was always in a dilemma whether to wear it down as the bob (which always looked lovely) had great movement to it. But after about half an hour in a hot, sweaty club, after a few backflips and a sidesplit, it could become very lank and lacking any body or movement.

Fortunately for me, this was the peak of the fashion for hairgel and gel spray. This is where my quaffed pony would come in. All I've got to say is Wella, Wella, Wella, ooh! This was my favourite brand; once you were gelled, dried and sprayed, your hair was set. Not only for the night, it could have gone a week – not that I ever did, of course. But regardless of which style I wore, it would always start with a wash, condition and blow-dry. Now, this would take a good hour or two, or three, as I'm sure many of you girls and gays know. If it didn't go right the first time round, I would have to repeat the whole process.

Taking all this into consideration, the hair could take three hours and there were only three hours left before we could no longer get free entry. I hadn't even started on spot squeezing, TCP-ing and a light covering of tinted moisturiser. But we always managed to make it, by hook or by crook, or by flirting with the big, chunky doorman if we happened to be a bit late.

But on this particular night, we were on time and there was a long queue as usual. It normally took about 15 minutes to get in if you were at the back of the queue. When we arrived, I saw him at the front of the queue – a vision. Honestly, I could see all those little hearts bursting all over the place.

Who, I hear you ask. Piero. (Obviously I didn't know his name was Piero then.)

I didn't feel very confident approaching anyone. I know some of you may find that hard to believe now, but in my teens I was very self-critical, never thinking I was good enough. I never really believed anyone would be interested in me. This was only in my personal life: in dance, it was a different story, I was full of confidence. But I made my mind up that night; I was going to speak to this man who, just by looking at him, had made me miss a breath.

Normally the 15 minutes' queuing would pass quite quickly but this evening it felt like a lifetime. I was worried something would happen and we wouldn't get in on time. Neither Carmine nor I had enough money to get in; if we were thirsty at the club, we would drink tap water.

Don't worry, everyone, we got in and I was, as they say in *Flashdance*, going on a manhunt. I didn't know anything about this man and we hadn't even spoken but already my mouth was dry and my palms were sweaty.

It really was love at first sight. After circling the club I don't know how many times, there he was, my love who did not yet know he was.

HE WAS wearing white Levi 501s and a blue and white striped top; his hair was thick and jet black, his eyebrows beautifully shaped. His eyes were chocolate brown, framed by long lashes and he had a strong nose and full lips.

He was with two of his friends, who were not beautiful like him. I knew that he couldn't be English – I thought perhaps he might be Brazilian, Spanish or Italian. As I edged closer to them, I tried to work out where they were from but with Madonna playing in the background and a lot of gay men screaming and laughing, I couldn't make head nor tails of it.

Fortunately for me, although Carmine was born in Switzerland, his mother tongue is Italian and he also speaks

French, German and Spanish, so if anyone was going to work it out, it would be him. Carmine was much more confident approaching people than I was in those days and he didn't miss a beat when I asked him to find out where this guy was from.

He went straight up to him and before I knew it, I was being beckoned over and introduced to Piero. Thank God he was Italian and couldn't speak the language, because if he spoke English, I still wouldn't have been able to speak. My body felt as if it had turned to jelly and started to melt when he opened his mouth and began to speak broken English in his beautiful accent.

When you meet someone who doesn't speak English, you tend to overcompensate with your body language and shout a lot. I had to hold back because I didn't want to frighten him off. If I had ever wanted to backflip and high kick, this was the time.

Even though I was 21 and had been going to clubs since I was 14, I had never had a boyfriend. As I said earlier, I never felt confident about myself when it came to relationships. For some reason, the fact that he was Italian and spoke little English, and the only Italian I knew was *Ciao* and Spag Bol, made it easier as we had to make more effort to have a conversation.

The thing that always frightened me the most if I spoke to someone in a club was they might presume that I wanted to have sex with them. Although I had kissed a few guys and maybe had a little fondle, I had still never had sex, or slept naked in a bed with another man. But I felt as though I didn't have to worry about this with him, as it would take forever to get to that point in a conversation.

From that moment we spent the rest of the night together in the club just talking, neither one understanding what the other was saying. I think we were each waiting for the other one to make the first move – there were many nervous moments when we would look at each other and laugh, when there really wasn't anything funny going on. Other moments we would gaze longingly at each other, seeing who would hold the glance longest, before moving in for our first kiss. Thank heavens, he did! I would never have done it.

It was that kiss, you all know the one, the one with fireworks. For the first time I felt totally at ease – I didn't care who was around me or who might be watching. It just felt right – I'm sure I had the Ready Brek glow around me. After our passionate kiss that must have lasted 10 minutes without coming up for air and a lot of heavy breathing, we finally parted lips and looked at each other. There was no nervous laughter this time, just big warm smiles.

During the course of the evening, Piero explained that he had come to London so that he could be the person he wanted to be. It was not easy for him to live life as a gay man from a Catholic background, growing up in an Italian village.

He was the same age as me, just turned 21, and he had never been in a relationship or had much contact with gay men. To put it another way, I had got him fresh in. He invited me round to his flat the next day for pasta; this made me very happy. My worst fear was that he might ask me back that night. He wrote down his address in Tulse Hill – I had never been there. It took him about half an hour to explain to me that I needed to go to Brixton and then get on the 2A or 2B bus. The fact that he spent so long trying to explain it made me feel good – it must mean he really liked me and wanted to see me again. It was either that, or my gelled quiff and my leotard had worked a treat.

I went to his place the next day for pasta, which was unlike any other I had tasted. It was Spaghetti al Pomodoro, made by a real Italian – a far cry from the spaghetti hoops I was used to. After the spaghetti, it was Tiramisu for dessert and I decided to stop over the night. For some people this might seem their worse nightmare, but for me it was perfect. The fact that he shared his bedroom with his flatmate meant that even though I shared his bed, no hanky-panky went on, just a lot of very sweet and affectionate kisses and the wonderful sensation of two bodies touching for the first time. Young love is a wonderful thing.

As our relationship developed, these are some of the things I put in my diary. I thought I was dramatic now; maybe I've mellowed with age.

Monday, 16 October 1989
Here I am, all alone, feeling lost without the most special thing I have ever had, my love. I feel empty and hollow inside. I'm here doing what I love, but this new love which I have never felt is so strong, that without it, I am weak. My heart beats strong and hard when I think of it. I know this love will always be in my heart.

Saturday, 19 October 1989
said a very stupid thing, but I had a feeling, which was wrong, and if I'm not careful I will spoil this good thing which we have. It's because this is new and I don't know how to

cope with it. From this day on I will relax and enjoy this love.

Sunday, 20 October 1989
Went to Roof Gardens. Had an alright time. Piero looked beautiful and is very sweet.

Monday, 21 October 1989
Think again how I have been feeling and how Piero is, and it is me who has been changing, and this could make Piero change. Because Piero will react to me; if I am down, Piero will be pulled down and start to wonder if this is good. Get it together and think.

Thursday, 24 October 1989
Now I know it was my fault, because tonight was wonderful, it felt good. How it should be!!!

Friday, 25 October 1989
Had a lovely day, he is so sweet and his heart is on his sleeve.

Saturday, 26 October 1989
Went to Bang. Had a good evening with P. It becomes better every day.

Friday, 1 November 1989
Went to heaven with Piero. Had a good time. LHVM. (For those of you who can't decode it, that means Love Him Very Much.)

STILL GOT IT, NEVER LOST IT!

Tuesday, 12 November 1989

The evening was so special. Something happened between us. He was so gentle and sweet. I never believed that something like this was real. I have only ever seen it in a film. But no-one was acting. I'm so happy and in love, and he has something special inside. I know he does, I can feel it. He has a glow which only I can see.

When you're young, you can be so full of shit. It's amazing how life can toughen you up so you forget some of those wonderful moments.

10
Miss Saigon

So, there I was, passionately in love, but still no real work, just bits and bobs here and there. They weren't even dancing jobs, really; walking around Selfridges dressed up as Napoleon wasn't really what I had in mind when I left college but I had to pay the rent so it had to be done.

Pineapple has always been an important part of my life, from the early days rehearsing for *Bugsy Malone*, when I was 14, to auditioning for dance jobs, and doing classes every day, when I wasn't being Napoleon.

Pineapple was the dancer's mecca and I remember when I first arrived, I felt at home – everyone was in Lycra, spinning and high kicking. We all knew about Pineapple, that it was where the professionals that we used to watch on TV would rehearse.

I always tried to act cool when I first arrived as a 14-year-old, surrounded by men in Lycra and crop tops. I loved the Eighties – the dancewear did not leave much to the imagination. I was very excited about my first visit during rehearsals for *Bugsy Malone* and I was not disappointed. I realised that it would be a great place to meet professionals and find out about work. I recognised so many faces from TV, and I could not believe I was in the same room as them.

We would check the Pineapple noticeboard every day to see if any new notices had been put up for jobs. The problem I had always faced was my height; even though I could dance rings around some of my competition, the dance industry can be fickle and often we are judged not on our talent, but on our looks. Or, in my case, height, because my looks weren't that bad.

My height is another thing I get from Mum. Not that Dad's side of the family is overly tall, but to tell you the truth, some of Mum's relatives are bordering on Munchkin. Mum's sister, my Auntie Maxine, says she is four foot 10, which means she is four foot nine. Honestly, if there was a yellow-brick road, we would not look out of place on it, skipping off to Oz to ask the Wizard for a few extra inches.

As per usual, Carmine and I checked the audition board at Pineapple and there was an audition for a dancer/acrobat and no height restriction was specified. Carmine decided to opt out of this one as he didn't do acrobatics. It was for a new show coming into the West End.

Even though I was a versatile dancer, I didn't really want to dance in West End shows; I wanted to dance for pop stars like Madonna and Kylie, but that didn't seem to be happening and I couldn't afford to be choosy. I needed to work.

I took the details of the job and turned up on the day of the audition, at Pineapple, where all the auditions were held. It was in Studio 2, and for any of you who have watched the show *Pineapple Dance Studios*, it's the medium-size studio next to reception and looks out on to Langley Street.

When I arrived at Pineapple there were about 15 guys there for the audition and we did a fairly simple dance routine. I say simple, it was simple for me; at this point about four or five of the guys were eliminated. Then they asked to see our acrobatic tricks. I thought I would go last, or as near last as possible to check out the competition, so I would know what I had to pull out of the bag. I am so pleased I did; where my height might have been a hindrance before, it was my trump card this time.

The studio was not large and the guys who were left in the audition were not overly tall, but taller than me. When it came to do a tumble run (that's when someone does backflips in a line, one after the other), it was a bit more difficult for them, because they didn't have much room. They managed to fit in two or three backflips; not me. I think I fitted about nine in, with an open layout summersault on the end. It was like the Bugsy Malone auditions all over again. The summersault into splits worked for me every time. As I landed in the splits out of my summersault, I just felt as if the job was mine.

Normally after an audition you wait a day or two to hear whether or not you are successful. I was told there and then that I had got the job. This was going to be my West End debut in a brand new show called *Miss Saigon*.

Considering I didn't even have an agent, I was feeling quite pleased with myself that I had got into the original cast of a West End show. Whether it would be good or not, I couldn't tell, but at that point I didn't really care. It was going to be an Equity contract, which meant that I would get an Equity card so I could get other jobs. I wouldn't have to be a French soldier at Selfridges and I couldn't wait to tell the pick'n'mix managers at the Trocadero where they could shove their bonbons.

I got on really well with the assistant choreographer who had taken the audition, Maggie Goodwin, but as I soon found out in rehearsals, if she didn't like you, she would say you're nanty noo-na, darling! She had the most wonderful expressions and truly, she was camper than Christmas.

It was Maggie who told me that I would need to be at rehearsals at Drury Lane on Monday morning at 10 am prompt and I've never been late coming – I mean arriving – I'm always just on time. I was going to be signing up for a year in a Cameron Mackintosh show and earning proper money. I say earning proper money – I still didn't know what I would be earning, but it had to be better than pick'n'mix.

I was excited that I had got a job in the West End but I wasn't thrilled that it was in *Miss Saigon*; it was a new show that no-one knew anything about. But when I arrived at the Theatre Royal, Drury Lane on Monday morning, the moment I walked into the auditorium in this beautiful theatre, looked at the stage (which was massive) and then at the auditorium (which just went on forever), my eyes just kept going up and up.

You could smell showbusiness in the theatre; there was such a buzz. There were groups of people laughing, being over-expressive, over-theatrical. I know, very unlike me, so usually understated. I was in heaven – and I don't mean under the arches at Charing Cross where I met Piero.

But I felt a little bit intimidated – I say a little, I don't mean a little, a lot. I didn't know anyone, and these were all seasoned professionals; I later found out that every one of them had done a West End show, or two, or three.

All the Vietnamese (the show was about Saigon) were played by Filipinos; I later found out they were all famous in their own country. I could tell this just by the way these performers held themselves, and their self-confidence – it was clear this was a cast of amazing people. Before I had spoken a single word to any of them, I already felt privileged to be a part of this incredible cast.

From the back of the auditorium I heard a loud public-school voice. 'Right, everybody, take seats in the front of the auditorium!' in a very abrupt and crisp tone.

'Very good to see you all here. I'm your director – my name is Nicholas Hytner.' For those of you who don't know anything about theatre, he is now Sir Nicholas Hytner, and he is a very respected and renowned director. Come to think of it, he was then – I just didn't know it.

Then Cameron Mackintosh stood up and said his piece. I had imagined him taller and posh, but he wasn't either. He was very warm and friendly, and, considering this was his gig, it gave me confidence to see that the man at the top didn't seem like a wanker.

First days can be awkward and uncomfortable, but this was unlike any first day I had ever had. Everyone seemed to know everyone else, and I was the new kid in town. It didn't take long to find out that I was the youngest member of the cast. I was also the last in – they had already cast everyone a good month before. I was brought in as an acrobat for one of the dance numbers and also to be a swing.

When you're a swing in theatre, it doesn't mean you go both ways: it means you cover the roles of the other cast members, normally multiple roles. And I certainly had my work cut out. I covered 22 people; I played the American GIs and also the Vietcong – although I know I don't look very Asian, they had a great make-up artist who would whack some prosthetics on us. Sometimes, if we were really down on cast members, I would even play one of the girls in the background.

Rehearsals lasted six weeks and as the original cast members, we created everything. If it didn't work, we changed it. It was the hardest thing I had ever done up to that point, but I couldn't wait to get up every morning to go to rehearsals with these inspiring people.

Before I knew it, it was opening night. There was such a buzz among the cast and crew. We knew we were a part of something that would last a long time; it felt special. And after the first-night performance, we knew we had a hit on our hands. The audience stood up and screamed out 'More, more!', and it was like that every night. The great thing was, the longer we did the show, the easier it became. We could relax into our roles and have more fun with them, and we certainly had fun on and off stage. You see, in the theatre there can be a much bigger show backstage than the one on stage.

There was always some drama going on, good or bad. There was Gill, the lesbian at the stage door, who would be having trouble with her bisexual stripper girlfriend, and Nick Holder and Jimmy Johnson, who decided they wanted their dressing room to be en-suite and so kicked the walls down, through to the showers next door.

When I told Mum and Dad that I had a role in a new West End musical called *Miss Saigon*, they were very pleased for me. For them it was just a job that was going to pay me an income. My family did not come to the West End to go to the theatre. They had no idea how big Drury Lane Theatre was, or what it might mean to get into a West End show.

Most of what they knew about the business I was in they learned from me, and I did not make such a big hoo-ha about *Miss Saigon* to them. It's not that they were not proud of me, because they were brimming with pride, but it was more of a relief to them that I could support myself.

I was one less thing to worry about. My two elder sisters, Rennie and Tania, had two kids each and were divorcing their partners at the time so they were a much bigger priority for my parents, making sure that they had the support they needed and that the grandkids were being looked after.

ONE NIGHT my youngest sister Kelly came to see the show and she was planning to stay at mine. There was one small problem: although I didn't feel the need to tell my family I was gay, it was pretty obvious. I thought it was best to let her know, as I was still living with Carmine and Ivan, and there were a few artistic pictures around the flat, mainly of models by Bruce Webber – I suppose you could call them homoerotic.

I met Kelly at the tube station and as we walked through Covent Garden to the theatre, I said to her, 'Listen, if you don't already know, I'm gay.'

Well, you would have thought from the look on her face that I had told her I was straight. The strange thing was, she started to cry; I thought it should have been me, shouldn't it? She was just trying to steal my glory. When I asked her why she was crying, she said she didn't know, so I told her to stop and enjoy the show, which she did.

I told her not to tell Mum and Dad; not that I thought they would be bothered by it, but I didn't feel the need to state the obvious. What difference would it make if I told them or not? I was still the same person and it wouldn't change anything. That's how I felt about it and it wasn't like I was struggling with anything; I loved my life and loved being me. I didn't go home that much and I had spent the last six years of my life away. I felt as if my life had moved on so quickly and I had experienced so much in such a short time, especially when I was in *Miss Saigon*, mixing with those wonderful people.

But she did tell them, and two weeks later I received a letter from Mum and Dad in the post. Considering we spoke on the phone almost every day, I thought it was strange receiving a letter from them. It read in part:

Dear Louie,

I would dearly have loved to speak to you personally, but as we rarely see you, it has to be a letter. Kelly went around to Rennie's the other day, and she mentioned the conversation she had with you about being gay.

Louie, you couldn't expect her to keep this to herself. It's something all the family should know and understand. Well, Louie, I'm not going to sidetrack around it. You're still the same Louie we brought up and loved for 21 years.

Dad and I have known for a long time. We're sorry you took so long to tell us; I do wish you had confided in me. Dad and I love you more than ever, and we feel so upset that you have had to bear this on your shoulders for so long on your own, when Dad and I should have been there to help and support you when you needed it.

Dad said that now this is out, he would like to see you and speak to you, and perhaps a barrier that has been there for so many years at last will come down, and you can love one another as a father and son should.

You must have been tormented all those years, Lou; I feel very guilty that I haven't been there for you, Louie. I want you now, Louie, to feel very relieved and happy.

You have a great future ahead of you, and now you don't have anything in your way.

Go for it, Louie! I think, the truth be known, I've probably known for many years, even before you did, but it doesn't change a thing. You are you, Louie, and we are us; you are our son and very proud of it we are too.

You have brought so much joy in our life and never any trouble. I cherish more than ever the special relationship you and I have always had, and will share forever. Please don't ever feel you have let yourself or your family down. You have a great and fulfilling life ahead of you, Louie.

Please take it by the horns and enjoy every day. Life is too precious to pass by without taking all you want from it. I'm sure now we can have a better relationship as a family than ever.

I hope this causes you no embarrassment.

We love you, Louie.

Mum and Dad xxx

Actually, the letter didn't embarrass me in the slightest, but the one thing it did make me understand is the fact that they had taken it harder than me. I never felt under pressure or alone, and I didn't feel any distance from my family. I was very surprised when I read, 'I'm sure now we can have a better relationship as a family than ever.'

I realised that, while I was living such a wonderful life and doing what I wanted, with people I loved being around, unknowingly I had neglected my family. My life felt so distant from theirs, I really didn't think that they would be interested in what I was going to wear to go down to Heaven, or who had the best *grand battement* (that's a high kick) in the show, when they were all busy knocking out kids and going down the local on a Saturday evening.

That was their life and they loved it, but I just didn't want to be a part of it. Whenever I went home, nothing had changed; it was all so boring. What I realise now is that I was being selfish and actually, their lives, and what they were doing, was as exciting and as important to them as my life was to me. It's just that mine was covered in fairy dust.

But that's what you do when you're young, isn't it? You learn. And even though the letter I received from my parents was heartfelt and sincere, at the time I didn't want to respond in any way as I didn't really feel affected by the contents. Once again, looking back, I should have given them the time; I should have explained how I was feeling, but I did not want to miss out on one second of the life I was living. I didn't know when something amazing might happen, and in my eyes, at that time, nothing was going to change back home.

Maybe Mum and Dad had been to B&Q, and Dad had done the downstairs bathroom. How could that compare to me spinning around on the West End stage, living the life of Kylie?

Oh, to be young and selfish! But, as the saying goes, you live and learn. Deep down in my heart, I knew no matter what I did, or how I treated my family, they would always be there for me, as I would be for them. It was just a phase, thinking my life was so much more important than theirs – not the gay bit. That's not a phase, and if it is, it's a bloody long one.

OOH, I didn't tell you how much I was earning at such a young age, did I? It was about £400 a week, with no agent's fee to pay. I felt rich, knowing that money was going into my bank account each week. I remember just wanting to spend it all. If I didn't spend it, it just didn't feel right. It was no longer fish and chips from the chippy; we started going to the grill and bar across the road from the theatre. It was classier than the fish and chips; I say classy, it was just more expensive. But it felt good!

Back then, I thought I had it all: a job doing what I adored, a boyfriend (Piero and I were official – Piero and I hadn't moved on to anyone else) and money! Now, can you all think back to when you were 21? If you had all of this, would you really want to go home to talk about shitty nappies and divorces? Be honest: I don't think you would, so please don't frown on me. But, like a good claret, I get better with age.

Not only was I in a West End show, I was in the *best* West End show. All the West End Wendys wanted to be in it – it was a guaranteed long run. We had Lea Salonga as Kim, she was the lead. Ruthie Henshall was in the cast too, as a chorine then, but she understudied one of the leads. Jonathan

Pryce was also in the cast. I had no idea who he was at the time – I was too wrapped up in legwarmers and Lycra.

I was a baby, working with such an amazing cast, and I learned so much about theatre; how to behave as a professional, but more than anything, how to laugh. I had never laughed so much in my life. From the dressers to the wardrobe department, and obviously to the actors on stage, there were some amazing characters.

No-one could just tell a story along the lines of 'I went to Tesco's and got a pint of milk' – it would be, 'As I glided through the piazza in Covent Garden, Puccini blasting from the opera house, the sun glistened down, spreading a sheen of glorious, golden light that marked my path to the tender lights of Tesco's. On entering, I was greeted by the waft of cool, icy air as I passed through the fruit section, with the smell of the tropics; then there it was in front of me, glorious, full-fat cow's milk.' OK, I may have gone over the top a bit, but you get my drift. Nothing was plain and simple any more, it was all coated with theatrics, as was I.

Now, if I wasn't on – and when I say on, I mean performing as I was a swing; if the whole company was on, then I had a night off I still had to stay in the theatre and I would often hang out with Gill, the lesbian on the stage door, and her two goldfish (I can't remember their names). We would go through her lesbian dilemmas – I didn't have much interest in it, but we would have a cup of tea and a B&H. Yes, I know, disgusting – I smoked then. I thought it was really big and really clever. I never did like it, and it didn't suit me and no, I don't do it any more.

I was also very friendly with the girls in wardrobe, as I would often come in early to wash my outfit for the disco.

Alison, one of the girls in wardrobe, was also our dresser and a diva on the sewing machine. It was amazing what she could do with a bit of cotton Lycra – I could have a new top every night, if I wanted. I was still going out every night and Carmine would come to meet me at the stage door. By this time we didn't have to worry about the flyers to get in for free, as we could afford to pay. If I was feeling very flush, I would have a half a lager shandy, thank you very much. It was no longer a glass of tap water from the bathroom.

Piero would normally meet us at Heaven because he was now working in the daytime, at Jigsaw, a clothing store in Covent Garden, and I was working at night, so the only time we got to see each other was after the show each night. It was awful because I couldn't bear not seeing him; I wanted to see him every day, but I couldn't. He started work at 8.30 in the morning so some nights he wouldn't come to meet us.

I can remember sometimes not wanting to be in Heaven and wanting to be with Piero, but it just wasn't possible. We both had flatmates and it wouldn't have been fair on them. I just had to remind myself how wonderful my life was at that moment and not to become obsessed with one person, which isn't as easy to do with your first love, as I'm sure you all know.

I HAD been in *Miss Saigon* nearly a year and my contract was up for renewal. Now, there wasn't anything else happening; I could have gone out into the world of commercial dance and *Top of the Pops*, but that's what Carmine was doing, and he wasn't working all the time.

I was being paid regularly and enjoyed being in the theatre. The other thing was, if I re-signed for another year, I would also get a salary increase. 'Could it get any better?', I hear you all asking? Quite frankly, no; so I decided to re-sign for *Miss Saigon*.

Some cast members decided not to, but they usually had other shows to go to. I wasn't bored, and I was happy, so it seemed the right thing to do. I told Maggie, the assistant choreographer, that I would like to re-sign for another year and she was pleased. I think she liked having me around because some of the cast weren't great dancers, although they were amazing singers.

I had made my decision. That night I was staying at Piero's. I used to get the bus near Waterloo Bridge with another girl in the cast, who lived in Tulse Hill, just down the road from Piero. The journey took about 40 minutes. I couldn't wait to tell him. One, because I had been asked to re-sign; even though I said some people wanted to leave, not everyone had been asked to re-sign, and two, I wanted to tell him that I was going to stay on in the show.

But when I arrived at Piero's, my world fell apart.

11
When in Rome . . .

Before I had the chance to tell Piero my good news, he told
me that he was going back to Italy. His father wasn't well
and he didn't know how long he would go back for.

I had to ask myself if he had really said that; I couldn't
believe the perfect life I was living had just been shattered. At
that moment I realised how much I loved him, and of course
there were tears.

I felt so sad for him, because I knew how much he loved
his life in London and how restricted he would be back in
Italy. It was not like I could get on a train and visit him; I felt
very uncertain about what was going to happen but I could
not let him see my insecurities, as his reasons for going back
were far more important.

Within two days Piero had returned to Italy. I had
never felt so much heartache – there seemed to be nothing
that could bring a smile to my face. I became moody and
grumpy, and all I spoke about was Piero and how much I
missed him.

Poor Carmine! When you are so wrapped up in your own story it's hard to see how boring it can be for everyone else around you. But that's what friends are for, and also to tell you to shut up – to live your life – because that's the point it got to with us.

A month had passed and there was no sign of Piero coming back soon, and I still had not signed for the next year of *Miss Saigon*. And I didn't sign for the next year: I had spoken to Piero and asked him if he wanted me to come to Italy, and he said yes. He didn't know how it was going to work, as we had nowhere to live; he was still living with his parents to look after his father. He couldn't explain to them why his friend was coming from London to live with him, and we couldn't stay in the village, so it meant that he would have to live in Rome.

Even though I was earning a lot of money, as I said, I was spending it too and I had only managed to save £3,000, and that wasn't going to last me long. It took a couple of days, but Piero finally explained to his parents that a friend of his was coming over and that he was going to help me out. So he would come to Rome, we would live with his sister and try to find somewhere to live together.

WHEN YOU'RE young and in love, nothing can stop you. But I had to do one thing before I moved to Italy; I had to tell Maggie that I would not be signing for another year. She was very sweet and understanding. I really did wear my emotions on my sleeve and everyone could see how sad I was. Even though she was also sad to see me go, she said I could always come back as long as the show was running. This gave me a sense of security and reassured me that I had made the right decision to move to Rome.

I still had that voice inside me saying, 'You won't get this chance again, don't mess up this opportunity; if you are meant to be together, you will be together.'

Mum and Dad were once again pleased that I was doing what I wanted to do. As long as I was happy, they were happy. My sisters were providing all the drama of marriage and divorce and breeding, so my long holiday to Italy didn't register as something for them to worry about.

Piero had met Mum and Dad a few times when they came to visit me in London and they liked him. They knew that we both cared very much for each other and they had accepted him as part of the family. At this point I was the only one in a stable relationship – with no kids, may I add – and they knew I was making the right decision to go to Italy to be with Piero. But once I had made my decision, all my fear and excitement turned to a feeling of adventure.

The furthest I had been was Majorca when I was about 12. The thought of going to Rome was so glamorous, so fashionable! What was I going to take with me? For some reason I felt that cut-off denim shorts and crop tops wouldn't be such a big thing in Piazza di Spagna, but I slipped them in my bag anyway.

I went to Rome in April, 1991 (I remember because Piero and I both have our birthdays in April). So it was a summer wardrobe to start off, and I assumed that the Italian summer would last longer than ours, plus a few woollies in case I was there for the winter.

While packing, I continually asked myself if I was making the right decision: I only had £3,000, and I was leaving an amazing job to go to another country. I didn't speak the language and I would have nowhere to live; I also considered that I might bump into the Italians I used to live with, the coke dealers. I didn't know where they were from, so it could have been Rome; I thought they probably weren't too happy with me flushing their drugs down the toilet. Eventually, common sense kicked in and I reassured myself that wouldn't really happen.

I packed my bags and rechecked for any leftover drugs; I thought, that's all I need, one rogue wrap to be left as I go through Customs. I suppose I would have got a good frisking, which is always nice from a man in uniform. But it was all fine and everything went smoothly; I got to the airport on time, and through Customs without a frisking. Three hours later and I would be with Piero in Rome.

I really felt I was on an adventure once I boarded the plane. There were so many Italians around me and I sensed that I would fit in well in Italy. They were all gesticulating theatrically and every time they spoke, it was like there was a big drama going on, when really all they were doing was ordering a cappuccino.

I was going to have to up my game with the gesticulating out there if I was to be noticed. Then I heard those wonderful words, 'Cabin crew, please take your seats – 10 minutes to landing.' Even though it was Italian and I couldn't understand a word, I knew what he was saying, as I could hear the landing gear being lowered.

The closer I got to seeing Piero, the faster my heart beat, until I thought it was going to explode. You know when you arrive at an airport, there's always a corner to turn into Arrivals, or those smoked automatic glass doors. At the airport in Rome they had smoked glass doors. I was almost there, just seconds away. Bang! The doors opened and everything seemed in slow motion; I seemed to be the only one moving, the rest was a blur. Such a feeling of joy and happiness went through my entire body when I finally saw Piero in the crowd.

WE HAD a big hug and a kiss on the cheek. All my senses seemed heightened – it was as if I had never touched him before and just the scent of him was amazing. We were so happy to see each other and now the adventure began in earnest.

Piero had driven to the airport and now I saw the smallest car I had ever seen. They were very popular in Italy, a Fiat Cinquecento, and I could just about fit my bags in the back. It was so strange being in a car with Piero at the wheel, because I had never seen him drive. He seemed so grown-up and manly – it made me feel quite the little lady.

There seemed to be no order to the way people drove in Italy; they were all over the road, beeping, cutting across, shouting, and I had never seen so many Vespas in my life. People were riding on the pavement – two up, three up! Everything seemed so old, from the ancient buildings to the bumpy roads, especially in a car half the size of a Mini.

Our destination was Piero's sister's flat. She was a student of architecture and shared with two others. I remember thinking that was very posh; my sisters worked in the poster factory and then they became pregnant.

His sister lived in an apartment block, about four storeys high. The entrance was clean and smelled very fresh; it was clad in marble. When we got inside, it seemed very cold and unhomely. Everything in the flat was marble and it all seemed sparse – I was used to curtains and carpets, and big sofas.

I discovered, with time, that carpets and heavy curtains and a Draylon sofa didn't really work in a hot climate. Piero's sister and her flatmates seemed very nice and were very hospitable, even though I couldn't understand a word they were saying. Piero and I ended up sleeping in their sitting room. It was strange, because we were so used to showing affection to each other when we wanted to, back in London. I felt on edge, in case we were caught kissing or whatever. Piero hadn't told any of his family that he was gay, although it was clear his sister knew; she just didn't speak about it.

Then Piero dropped the bombshell, that we could only stay with his sister for a week. My understanding had been that we could stay there as long as we wanted, until we had found somewhere to live. At that moment, even though Piero was my world, I questioned myself whether or not I had made the right decision. Even though I was with the most important person in my life, at that time I felt so lonely; I didn't speak Italian and he had not had time to look for anywhere for us to stay.

IT IS amazing when you have to do something that seems against the odds; the next morning I knew I had to find a place for us to live. Piero was distracted by caring for his parents and dealing with their constant questions about why he wanted to be in Rome with his friend.

My first port of call the next day was to find a dance centre; although I didn't speak the language, I understood the language of dance. I knew it had to be the same as in any major city – it wasn't what you knew, it was *who* you knew. I had to find out if there was any work, or any auditions.

I got Piero to find out where the dance centre was and we went there on his sister's Vespa. It was an amazing journey; we did not wear helmets and it felt very exciting riding through the streets of Rome, dodging cars, riding on the pavement. I saw people on every corner, drinking coffee, in cafes. We did the same – hopped off the Vespa to have a coffee on the way to the dance centre. It was a real song and dance: the language sounded so musical and people were so passionate.

There wasn't a grey suit in sight: the men were very expressive in their fashion. There were a lot of pastel colours, which threw my gaydar completely off. Not only did the women greet you with a kiss, the men did too. We only did that in London down Old Compton Street with the other gays. Everyone was at it in Rome – the men walked arm in arm down the street. Piero had to tell me that it didn't mean they were gay, it was just what Italian men do. I remember thinking to myself, maybe that's why the Pope wears a dress.

Once I got my gaydar back on track, we made our way to the dance centre. It was called 'Jazz', but was pronounced 'Yazz' and was similar to Pineapple, with fewer classes: you paid an entrance fee and paid the teacher in the class. I got Piero to ask if there was a lyrical jazz class and an audition board, and the answer was yes, to both questions.

There was a jazz class at 4 pm that afternoon; the best thing for me was to go to the class, meet some people and find out what was going on workwise. We had a quick look at the audition board before leaving and there was only one: for dancers for a TV show. The audition was taking place about a week later.

We went into the centre of Rome to buy some clothes so that I could take class that day and we stopped for lunch near the Trevi Fountain. Honestly, it was like being in a Fellini movie. I was Anita Ekberg, but stayed out of the fountain. I didn't have time for a kick around in the water – I had to get back to do a dance class.

When I got back to Jazz, Piero left me and I felt a little bit scared because I didn't speak the language, but I felt safe in that environment. I can laugh about it now, but dancing can be very territorial. As at Pineapple, if you do a class every day, you tend to stand in the same place, even if it's an open class. I quickly figured out that it must be the same at Jazz, but I worked out from the gesticulations and the looks of complete disgust that I was in somebody's spot. I remember thinking, what a bitch, but I couldn't fight with them verbally; but God knows this bitch had it coming to her when it came to the *grands battements* and pirouettes.

When you are new in a dance class, especially a professional class, people look at you to see what kind of warm-up you do, how loose you are, or how high you could get your legs. I decided to give nothing away, but looked to see who the divas were in that class.

First, I wanted to check out the competition, and secondly, I wanted to know who I would have to speak to about getting a job. There were about three or four of them in class; I could see that one guy in particular was going to be amazing, and he was.

As I was at the back of the class, no-one could see what I was doing, but I could see all of them. I wasn't going over the top, wrapping my legs around my neck, even though I could; I was leaving everything very centred and placed, until we got to going across the floor. Once you have done your warm-up in the centre, you cross the room diagonally, doing jumps, kicks and pirouettes. Once again, I put myself at the back of the line so I could see the competition going before me.

The guy who I spotted earlier was first in line; being first in line was always a good spot. It meant the whole class watched you and no-one got in your way. Being at the back could also be a good spot because everyone had been, and they could then watch you. I was right about the bitch whose spot I had taken in class: she was awkward, with bad technique, and couldn't pirouette to save her life.

It was nearly my turn to go across the floor. I had to get it right if I was to make an impact and get in with the right people. The combination was kicks and pirouettes, movements I had mastered in class with Theresa back in London and Cambridge.

I kicked ass! My legs were around my ears, and I was knocking out eight pirouettes both sides. It's amazing how you can start a class not knowing anyone, spend a whole hour doing a warm-up with not even a look, and yet, it only takes 30 seconds to have the whole class wanting to be your friend.

The dancer I noticed earlier came up and introduced himself to me; his name was Julianino. Fortunately for me, he spoke English. You normally find that, don't you? Most foreign people speak a bit of English, but the English mostly speak English.

After class we went for a coffee and he told me about an audition that wasn't listed on the audition board, but was a very good job. In fact, it was one of the best jobs a dancer could get in Italy. It was for a TV show called *Fantastico*, which was their lottery show, but it was nothing like ours. It was a big variety show; it lasted for three months and they had amazing star guests from around the world to perform on it.

The choreographer was Franco Miseria, who was popular with all of the dancers: everyone wanted to work for him. Julianino told me that I would need to get a dance piece together to audition for the show. I found this strange, as in London the choreographer would normally set the piece. But, as they say, when in Rome, do as the Romans do.

WHEN PIERO came to meet me after class we went straight to HMV in the centre of Rome and I bought Mariah Carey's album, *Emotions* – her first album, which had come out the same year, in 1991.

We then went to Piero's sister's flat, where I listened to the album. I decided I would dance to 'Vision of Love'. Don't ask me how, but I choreographed a routine in the front room of the flat. This was quite difficult, as I could never do it full out – there just wasn't the space.

On the day of the audition for the TV show Piero dropped me off at the dance centre and then made his way to work (he had found a job in a clothes shop a couple of days before, just by the Piazza di Spagna). He wished me luck and left me to my fate.

Once inside, it was a typical audition situation, with the good dancers huddled together and the tryers at the end, hanging on to every word they were saying. All I got when I went in was deathly stares. It was very strange to me because whenever I auditioned in London, I was the one who knew everyone. Here I was just the outsider, the foreigner.

Unfortunately Julianino wasn't at the audition; he had a job in Paris, but he had told me to tell the choreographer that I was his friend and that he had told me to audition. I would have, too, if I could have got anywhere near him. It was like he was some kind of god. He walked in to the studios, threw his arms around a bit and sat down. Then we launched into a long warm-up, which was also different to London, where you would normally warm up by yourself before an audition.

I couldn't believe it, but even in the warm-up they already started eliminating people. I knew there was no way I could afford to be kicked out of the audition: I had to get the job so I could stay with Piero in Rome. The small amount of money I had was not going to last long and it wasn't enough to get an apartment in Rome. I managed to get through the warm-up without being kicked out. I couldn't figure out if it was because I was good, or that the choreographer couldn't see me at the back.

At the end of the warm-up he lined up the girls and pointed along the line, saying '*Si, non, si, si, non*'. I thought, you have got to be kidding; now he's just lining people up and kicking them out. It was no joke – that was exactly what he was doing.

All the boys lined up, and the same again, 'Yes, no, yes, yes, no'. As he got closer to me, I was willing in my head, '*Si, si*'. When he got to me, it was a 'no'!

There was absolutely no way that I was going to leave that room without him seeing me dance. I remember thinking, what a complete knob! Who does he think he is, getting rid of people when he hasn't seen them dance, just in warm-up?

I don't know where it came from, but I just said, no, I'm not going. By the look on his face you would have thought someone did their business on his table. He started to throw his arms around, shouting in Italian, and looked pretty pissed off. But this wasn't a life or love situation for him as it was for me.

Fortunately for me, his assistant, Ranco, spoke perfect English and explained to me that what he was saying, with his arms flailing, was that I was no good for the job because I was too short. I refused to back down and asked her to tell him that he hadn't seen me dance. He replied that he didn't need to see me dance, he had made up his mind – he was Franco Miseria.

I told Ranco, I don't care if he's fucking God, I ain't leaving! I don't think she gave him a direct translation, but he stood up from his chair, pointed at me and shouted '*Musica, musica!*'

Ranco told me to give him my music – he would see me dance now. I had to squeeze my sphincter quite tightly at this point, as I thought I might actually shit myself. Not only had I created this huge scene, I would now have to dance in front of everyone. I had never done the routine flat out, as there wasn't enough space in Daniella's flat.

The next minute was going to make all the difference between my staying in Rome with Piero and going home with a broken heart. I know, it's dramatic, but it was.

If I do say so myself, I kicked ass. The whole room erupted in applause when I finished, and I was offered the job there and then. I had arrived in Rome.

12

La Dolce Vita

The job was going to start in October and we were still in May. I couldn't believe it! I had the job, but what use was it to me? I needed the money now – we had to get an apartment. I explained that I needed a job now or I wouldn't be able to afford to stay in Rome, and would have to go back to London.

After a bit of to-ing and fro-ing with Ranco translating for us, this godlike choreographer, who until now I had thought was a total wanker, said he would lend me money until the job started. Not only that, he knew of an apartment in the centre of Rome that I could move into. It was owned by the TV channel. I couldn't believe it! I was right from the beginning: he really was a god!

So, in the space of three hours, I had an apartment and the money to pay for it, and I could spend the whole summer having a holiday.

Things could only get better. Within a week, Piero and I had moved into the apartment in Via Goito, above a wine shop called Trimanni. There was already a dancer living in the apartment and she also worked for the TV channel. She was very pretty, and also spoke English, which was great for me. The apartment was amazing: it had two large wooden doors, with a smaller door set in, through which you entered the building. There was an ornate lift in the building and the floors in the apartment were parquet.

The furniture was dark, solid wood, and there were floor-to-ceiling windows that opened on to balconies. I knew then I had made the right decision to move to Rome.

I know you must be thinking that it couldn't get any better, but it really did. Piero took the morning off work to come and sign the TV contract with me because I couldn't read it. He read through it, and they were offering me 'three' a week. I was on at least £400 a week in London on *Miss Saigon*. This was their biggest TV show, but I have a motto, 'You don't ask, you don't get', so I told Piero that I wanted the Italian equivalent in lira of £500. I thought they might come back with £400, that's how it normally works with negotiations. As you can imagine, there were a lot of arms being thrown around, but they agreed on five. Piero had a smile from ear to ear. I thought, yes, it's good – I have done well.

I told Piero that I thought they would stick at £300. I wondered why he was looking at me open-mouthed at what had just happened. He explained to me that they weren't offering me £300, it was 3,000,000 lire, which worked out at about £2,000 per week.

That's why the arms had been thrown around so much! I had just got them up to five, which worked out at about £4,000 per week. I couldn't believe it. Knowing I had this money to come and the rent was being paid (although I would have to pay it back once I started earning on the show), I was left with about £2,400 for the next four months and Piero had a job as well.

IT ENDED up being one of the best summers of my life. They really did have summer in Italy – the sun was out every day. There was a beach about an hour away from Rome, by train. It was at Ostia, and when you arrived you would take a bus along the beach and get off at the last stop. After walking for a mile you would arrive at il Bucco, which means the hole.

This was a first for me as well. It was a gay beach, and I hadn't seen anything like it in my life. You didn't get this in Bognor. There were gorgeous men and women, and men-women, who had it all upstairs and down. For a Catholic country, they really did have it all, especially on the beach. To top it all, you could bronze every bit of your anatomy if you wanted to, because it was also a nudist beach. It was amazing. Everyone was hanging out, literally, on the beautiful clean sandy beach. You could see fish in the clear water and after a day of bronzing, the music would start to play at the beach bar and everyone would begin dancing.

I really felt as if life couldn't get any better – I had to keep pinching myself. I felt as if I were starting to grow up then: I was doing all of these things on my own and I felt that I could do anything. In London I was always dependent on someone else; in Rome I had a sense of achievement and I felt strong. I was ready to take on the world and any challenge that might come my way.

One big challenge I had to try and master was the language. As you may already know, I was not academically engaged. I wasn't about to attend night school to learn the language correctly: I decided I would learn it from the people around me and speak the current language.

The gender distinctions in the language confused me; for some reason I spoke in the feminine but everyone understood me. I could only just speak English: I didn't know how I was going to master Italian, but I didn't have a choice. If I wanted to get through the day, I would have to speak the language.

I mastered it eventually and things got easier when I started rehearsals for *Fantastico*. We were in the studio for eight hours each day and I had no choice but to learn, or I wouldn't have understood what was happening. I don't know if this is true for everyone learning a foreign language, but it all fell into place one day. I didn't have to think about what I wanted to say, or translate it first – I just said it in Italian.

The rehearsals were going well and I got promoted to *primo ballerino*. I must say, some of the Italian dancers weren't happy about it. *Primo ballerino* means first dancer, and it meant that I had more focus on me during the dances. But it was a big deal in Italy; maybe they thought they had better get their money's worth. There weren't any shows in England where dancers had such a presence. You were normally a backing dancer and that's exactly what you did, you stayed in the background.

In Italy everyone knew the dancers' names, especially on this show, which had massive viewing figures and also aired over the Christmas period. Things couldn't be more perfect. I had experienced a wonderful summer, I had a great

'ALREADY STRETCHING MY HAMSTRINGS.'

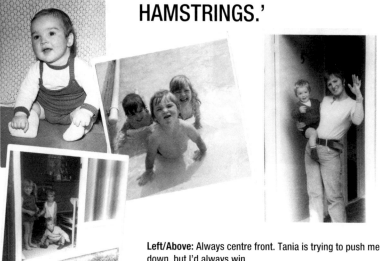

Left/Above: Always centre front. Tania is trying to push me down, but I'd always win.
Above right: Special time – Mum and me on our own.

Above Left: Looking clean and fresh after one of our shared baths. I don't think I peed in it that time.
Above: Mum's side of the family, headed up by Nanny and Grandad Lock, with Nanny Downer far left.

Above: One of our wonderful holidays at Butlins. Mum doesn't look too happy – she was most probably pregnant again.

'DID I REALLY NEED TO SAY ANYTHING? I DON'T THINK SO, DO YOU?'

Middle: Tania, Rennie and me all modelling the same hair thanks to Mum and her wallpaper scissors.
Above: My baby sister Kelly and me. Mum had got some new scissors, so we now had layers.

Left: Me looking bored on the end. My first taste of the military, but not my last!
Below: I always loved a good crop top.

Above Left: Mum looking very proud of Dad's handiwork, with our new porch and brick wall, outside 19 Goldingham Drive.
Left: Dad co-ordinating his look with our orange leather sofa and 70's shag-pile carpet.

Left: Nanny and Grandad Lock, always smiling.
Below Left: Nanny and Grandad Twinkle with Twinkle the dog.
Below: Mum and Nanny Downer in her warden-controlled flat.

Left: Nanny Downer, Kelly, Mum, Tania and me on holiday on the Isle of Wight.
Above: Rennie, Tania and me dining al fresco at 19 Goldingham Drive.

'TYING MYSELF IN KNOTS IN EXCITEMENT OVER MY FIRST PAIR OF BATTY RIDERS.'

'A COUPLE OF POSES INSPIRED BY FREEMANS CATALOGUE.'

'MY WEST END DEBUT IN *BUGSY MALONE* AT HER MAJESTY'S THEATRE, HAYMARKET.'

BUGSY MALONE ON STAGE

CAST LIST

Bugsy	WAYNE GODDARD (14)
Blousey	RACHEL AYNSON (13)
Fat Sam	LEE CHAPPELL (15)
Tallulah	GAIL MCLEAN (13)
Dandy Dan	STEVEN MACKINTOSH (16)
Knuckles	MISS MOLLOY (16)
Fizzy	SCOTT SHERMAN (11)
Leroy	MARTIN WALLACE (15)
Cagey Joe	PATRICK HENRY (15)
Bangles	TAMMY NEEDHAM (12)
Lorelei	SAMANTHA WAKDEN (13)
Roxy Minton	BENJAMIN HORRIS (13)
Babyface	PAUL HANDS (13)
Captain Smolsky	MICHAEL QUILL (13)
O'Dreary	GAVIN FORWARD (11)
Lena	RACHEL PITTMAN (14)
Bonnie	MATTHEW MELLA (13)
Lefty	PHILIP NEVILLE (13)
Butter	JEREMY BOOKER (14)
Louie	JEFF WHITE (12)
Doodle	JONATHAN DUX (11)
Yonkers	JAMES REILLY (13)
Bronx Charlie	JEFFREY CROSSLAND (13)
Laughing Boy	JULIAN KALPHAUS (13)
Shoulders	ALASTAIR NATSS (15)
Snake Eyes	LOUIE SPENCE (14)
Tillie	MAXINE NICHOLLS (14)
Dotty	LUCY DALE (14)
Mindless	AISLING REYNOLDS (11)
Hooker	JACEY CLARK (14)
Dancer	SOPHIE LAWRENCE (11)
Dancer	SARAH CHAPMAN (13)
Dancer	LORRAINE MEACHER (13)
Dancer	TONI SPAKINS (12)
Dancer	ABIGAIL ANDREWS (13)
Lucine	COLIN DOWNING (13)
Jelly	MARK BOYNTON (13)
Candy Girl	JOANNE-FLEUR BYRETT (11)
Singer	SAMANTHA VINNELL (15)
Flower Girl	KARINA PHILLIPS (11)
Policeman	PAUL VARNEY (12)

This Company will appear at all performances during the period 21.12.83 – 31.12.83 inclusive and 9.1.84 – 11.2.84 inclusive.

```
TELEMESSAGE LXP                                    21 December 1983
LOUIE SPENCE            BLACKSMITH
ROOM 223
THE IVANHOE HOTEL
TOTTENHAM COURT ROAD
LONDON W1


        GOOD LUCK ON YOUR FIRST NIGHT LOUIE. ALL OUR LOVE

    MUM DAD AND GIRLS
```

'YOU COULDN'T BEAT A WEDGE HAIRCUT IN THE 80S. THERE'S NOTHING LIKE A GOOD FLICK.'

Below/Right: Dadina, Yvonne and me hanging out in Braintree town.

Above: Rennie and Dad on the floor, while I got the chair – all watching a blank TV screen. Times were hard!
Left: Me at the ballet bar, accessorising. There's nothing like a good hoop earring.

LEFT: 'I DID TRY – IT JUST **DIDN'T WORK**.'

'MY FIRST REAL LOVE, PIERO. OH, TO BE YOUNG AND IN LOVE!'

Left: Me and the boys from *Miss Saigon* – don't know how Joan Collins got in there.

Right: Hanging out at Goodge Place with Take That, as you do.

'GETTING ALL SPICED UP – ME AND VB, AND MY FAVOURITE OF THEM ALL, MY WIFE IF I WAS STRAIGHT: MY DARLING EMMA.'

Below: A 5, 6, 7, 8… a quick snapshot in between studio checks at Pineapple.
Left: Me dressed as a baby for Emma's rendition of 'Baby Love' at Wembley Stadium, '98.

Right: I'm telling you, it was that big! Oh, you wanted my score? Sorry, Christine.

job, and things between Piero and me couldn't have been any better.

At least I *thought* things couldn't get better between us. I had decided to stay with Piero in Rome after my contract with the TV show ended on 6 January (Franco Miseria had already told me there was more work he would like me to do in the New Year). But everything changed one evening when I returned to the apartment after doing the show.

It was cold, for Italy; it was dark and wet, and I looked forward to getting back to our warm apartment. Piero would normally have cooked some wonderful pasta, but this evening, as soon as I walked into the apartment, I sensed that something was different. The apartment felt cold: the TV was off, and no lights were on, except for one in the kitchen.

Normally he would be cooking for me, especially his *sugo* (pasta sauce), but there was nothing on the stove. My first thought was that his dad must have taken a turn for the worse. I went straight into the kitchen, where I found Piero sitting next to the cooker, with his head hanging down. I asked him what was wrong, but he kept shaking his head. I asked him if it was his dad, but he said no. I couldn't figure out what could make him feel that way.

Finally he looked up at me, shaking his head, and said that he had been unfaithful.

13
Take That

I was literally speechless: I tried to speak, but nothing came out of my mouth. As quickly as the life left me, it came raging back through my feet, boiling up through my legs, through my belly, which was turning rapidly, and my heart beat so fast I felt as if I had just run a marathon. My head felt as if it were going to explode. I don't think I had ever been so angry and upset; I couldn't believe it, it was too much to take in.

'What have you done?' I started to scream at him at the top of my voice. 'What have you done?'

He just sat in front of me with his head lowered, shaking his head without speaking. I just wanted to know what had happened and why. He didn't reply, and it was all too much for me. I felt I was going to hit him, or smash something else. Even though I wanted to hurt him, I just couldn't.

I picked up the saucepan that was on the cooker and I started to smash up the kitchen. At this point he looked up at me with a look of dread on his face, but I couldn't stop.

The feeling of release was too strong – I had to let my anger out.

When I stopped smashing around the kitchen I collapsed in a sobbing heap against the wall and slid down on the floor, sobbing and asking repeatedly, why, why, why? Twenty minutes before, my life was perfect, and now I felt completely isolated without friends and family. Piero had become my complete life, my total being, and now I felt I didn't know him. I was alone in a foreign country with no-one to turn to.

Even though the thought of him with someone else was killing me, I needed to know every detail. Looking back now, it doesn't make any difference. Nothing would be changed by it, but at the time, I thought knowing who, why and where would make all the difference.

I was so hurt and I spent the whole night crying, while Piero tried to comfort me. I couldn't bear to have him near me or touching me. I thought about everything I had given up for him without thinking of it – my family, my friends, and my wonderful job. I couldn't understand how someone could do this to me, someone I loved, and who, I thought, loved me.

After a sleepless night I had made up my mind to fly back to England on 7 January, a day after the show ended. One good thing that had come out of this was that I had some money in the bank and I wouldn't have to worry about work. I would also be able to afford a flat.

The last month in Rome was difficult. We decided to try and work our way through this episode, but I would still go back to London. Piero would have to stay in Italy while his father continued treatment for his illness. He did not know when he might be able to return to London.

I had to be brave and stick to my guns, and not go back on my words; I had to go back to London. Even though I had never felt pain like this before, I still loved Piero, and wanted to be with him. I needed to know that he felt the same way. If he loved me and cared for me, he would show me while I was in London that he regretted what he had done. I needed him to prove to me that he really did love me. If I stayed in Italy, it might have seemed that it was all OK. I had to show that I had some control in the relationship; it was not about playing games.

WHEN I returned to London I stayed with Carmine for a couple of weeks. He had moved on from Finsbury Park and was living in the West End, near Tottenham Court Road, in Percy Street. I decided that was where I wanted to live.

I found a flat just down the road from him, number 15 Goodge Place. It wasn't a flat, more of a bedsit, with separate kitchen and bathroom. The studio room was split by sliding doors and it was fine for me on my own while I waited for Piero to come back.

Everything seemed to go well; we spoke on the phone every day and he sent me beautiful letters. None of us is perfect, and we all make mistakes. He came back to London in April and we had been apart for nearly four months. In that time we realised that we still wanted to be with each other. We stayed together for another seven years. Even though I tried hard not to let this episode affect our relationship, looking back, it definitely did. I never really trusted him again, and that innocent and pure love was never the same.

Louie Spence

We still had some great times together in Goodge Place; it was a hub of activity. Because it was so central, people were always dropping in to see us and to stay the night. True to her word, Maggie, the assistant choreographer on *Miss Saigon*, gave me my old job as soon as a vacancy came up on the show.

I stayed on and off at *Miss Saigon* for the next four years. In between contracts I would do the odd job here and there for pop acts including Boyzone, Björk, and a whole array of others. This was great for me, as it meant I was always working. I was fortunate that my versatility as a dancer meant that I could cross over from musical theatre to commercial pop.

I had a choice to sign on again for *Miss Saigon*, but I knew that there was a Take That tour coming up. I had never done a tour before and Take That were absolutely massive: every commercial dancer wanted to do that job in 1995. I had always been fortunate as a dancer – thanks to *Miss Saigon*, I was always working. I thought I should take a chance for the Take That tour, as it was something I wanted to do.

In Italy I had worked with big acts on *Fantastico*, artists such as Tina Turner, Ray Charles and Cindy Lauper. Talking to their dancers, they made touring sound so exciting. You were always meeting different people and dancing in front of massive audiences. And they didn't get much bigger than Take That.

I made my mind up that I would try for the audition and I did not sign up for *Miss Saigon* again. On the day of the audition at Dance Attic in Fulham, every dancer in the country seemed to have turned out. Fortunately for me, I was what you call 'in with the in-crowd'. Unlike when I was in Italy, having to scream and stamp my feet to be seen, I just queue jumped! One of my friends was assisting the choreographer on the audition. I suppose you could say I got fast-tracked.

It was bad enough that there were hundreds of dancers there; I had forgotten that Mum was coming up to London on the same day. At 9am she knocked on my door and ended up coming along to the audition with me. Thank God she didn't have her dancing tights with her or she would have tried to slip into the audition! I left her in the cafe area while I went through. They had already cleared out lots of people; because I had been fast-tracked, I just went in once they got down to the final 100. I was still in at the final 75 and the final 50.

At that point they took a break and we all went out to get a sandwich. When I left, I couldn't see Mum anywhere. I thought she must have gone to do a bit of shopping, but oh no. When I got back into the audition room, who was sitting in there like a pig in shit, chatting to Take That? Patricia Pamela Spence.

As you can imagine, I was mortified. There was the crème de la crème of the dance community and now my mum was sitting in on the audition. She wasn't at the table at the front – no, she was off to the side, with Jason from Take That.

Although she has never been a pushy, showbiz mum, I could see her pointing and laughing. I didn't know what to do. Should I go over there and say, 'What do you think you are doing?' To be quite honest, she and Jason looked as if they were having a whale of a time.

So I just went over and said, 'Mum, I've been looking for you everywhere. Don't you think you should go outside and wait in the cafe?'

To which Jason replied, 'No, she's fine, she can stay. We're having quite a nice time.'

I thought, great, I've given up my security and not signed on again for *Miss Saigon*, and my mum will end up getting the bleeding job.

I don't know what they were saying, or if hanging out with her new best friend Jason helped the situation, but I got the job. As you can imagine, I was as happy as Larry, working with the biggest band in Europe. I got the job that everyone wanted, working with five gorgeous boys. I was going to be huge with the gays and girls! The girl dancers started to rehearse a week before the boys for a number that they were doing with the band.

EVERYTHING WAS going swingingly: I was at home, with a lasagne in the oven. I had made the béchamel myself. I was known in West One for my cannelloni and lasagne. Those dishes were perfect for reheating, especially when guests dropped in, which they did constantly. We never used the microwave: Piero didn't like it. Italians are very precious about their food.

So there I was, ready to tuck into my lasagne, watching the early evening news on ITV. I wasn't really paying much attention to it, until I saw the boys flash up on the screen. By this time, they were 'the boys' to me, they were no longer Take That, even though I hadn't as yet set foot in the rehearsal studio.

Robbie was leaving! The first thing I thought was, how inconsiderate! I've told everyone I'm going to work with him. My second thought was, shit, will the tour go ahead?

There were phone calls between all the dancers, and one of the girls who was rehearsing with the boys when Robbie quit had heard that the tour *was* going ahead. I had to assume no news was good news; I even thought about ringing Pat. Maybe she had Jason's number and hadn't told me.

Any Take That fans who were around in 1995 can tell you the tour went ahead. Rehearsals were delayed by a couple of days and we started on the Wednesday instead of the Monday. I could feel the tension in the rehearsal studios on the first day. The boys were great, ultimate professionals who made us feel very welcome, even though it was obvious they were under a lot of pressure.

There was a lot of media attention because of Robbie's departure from the band, but they made it very clear that they were determined to make this tour better than their previous ones. This show wasn't technically difficult for the male dancers in the show; the girls had more to do as they were dancing with the boys as well. I made it clear I was more than happy to step in at any time, if required.

I wasn't a Take That fan, although I liked their music, and I don't think I fancied any of them. After working with them for a while, I decided that Howard was really hot. He had an amazing body and a great ass. Eventually, though, Gary became my favourite on the tour: he also looked amazing, his body was great, and he was very warm and funny with all the dancers.

He got so warm with one of them, Dawn, that he actually married her. Gary was very quick-witted and had the most amazing sense of humour. He was always a pleasure to be

Missed him on tour '95 but got him in the end.

around. With Dawn getting fairly friendly with him, we ended up going out together quite often, the three of us, along with another dancer on the tour: Lisa Jones.

It was the first time I had experienced real celebrity for a prolonged period. Gary used to pick us up at the hotel in his black Range Rover, which had blacked-out windows. He would take us out to dinner or to a club. From the moment we left the hotel car park, we were followed by cars and bikes, photographers snapping us at every traffic light. I thought it was quite funny – it all seemed very glamorous.

As you can imagine, the last thing Gary wanted was to be followed by paparazzi when he just wanted to go out with his friends. After a couple of months of hanging with the lads, I considered myself a friend.

One night, while we were in London, the boys came over to my flat at Goodge Place before we went on to a club. It was surreal, for real, believe me. When I looked out of my double-glazed sash window, I saw two large silver Mercedes vans with blacked-out windows and full security downstairs. As I said earlier, my cannelloni and lasagne went down a treat. The only problem was there weren't enough places to sit, with me, the boys, Piero, and some other dancers. I had a pull-down sofa in the sitting-room area, which was made of foam, with not much structure, and it collapsed easily beneath the slightest pressure. And that evening it had the biggest boyband in Europe on it – it must have collapsed at the thought of it alone.

Once we had finished my cannelloni, we moved on to a club, where there were more comfortable seating arrangements. It was another fun-filled night and two days later, there was a knock at the door. It was a delivery driver from Habitat, but I hadn't ordered anything, and neither had Piero when I went upstairs to check with him.

When I asked the driver what it was, he said it was a sofabed, in my name, with the correct delivery address. It had all been paid for. Along with it came a little card that said, 'Enjoy the new sofa. The one you have is shit. Love, Gary.'

Can you believe it? I didn't. How sweet was that? He had obviously thought about it – it wasn't just a sofa, but a sofabed. He had realised that if I had guests, they would need somewhere to sleep. I was very touched by his generosity and kindness. That's how he was, throughout the whole tour – and not just with me, but with all the dancers.

At Christmas, during the tour, he was staying at a hotel in central London and I met him for a drink. He had lots of gifts from lots of companies and he gave some of them to me, including aftershaves and clothes. It was great and we stayed good friends for a while after the tour. I often used to meet up with him, Dawn and Lisa when he had his flat in London.

After he moved up North we didn't keep in close contact, but whenever I see him and Dawn now, they are always very lovely. You are guaranteed that he is going to make you laugh with that dry wit and his great sense of humour.

14

Falling Out of Love

Things were great with my career: I was getting lots of commercial jobs, working with many different pop artists and doing some TV commercials. But during this time, my relationship with Piero had started to break down. It was not a sudden thing, but like many long-term relationships, we tried to pretend things were fine, when they were not.

It started in 1994, the year before I began the tour with Take That. We would argue about stupid things – the little things that don't bother you at the beginning of a relationship, but with time, start to grate on you. We would have an argument about something as petty as not washing up a cup; because of that, we might not speak for a couple of days, or a week. It didn't seem to bother either of us that we weren't speaking.

Eventually, living in such a confined space, it became harder and harder to ignore each other. I suppose the good thing was that my work gave us some respite, as I could be away for a couple of weeks or a month dancing. It is sad when you have loved someone that much and it is difficult to understand how it is that you can still love them, yet no longer be *in* love with them.

I knew that I was falling out of love with Piero, and he with me, but I also knew that we both desperately loved each other. We had grown up together and experienced so many things. I was nearly 20 when we met and we finally broke up eight years later.

The day I told him I wanted him to move out, I had bumped into him on Old Compton Street. We were in a period of not speaking, and I had no idea where he was. I had decided I couldn't take it any longer.

I felt anxious and sad when I saw him.

'Where are you going?' he asked.

I was so upset and I could not help showing it. 'I'm not going anywhere. I'm just walking around in circles, thinking about us. The way I'm feeling just isn't right. I still love you, Piero, but I don't think we are in love any more.'

He was silent, listening to me, so I took a deep breath. The tears were starting to come and I was choking up, but I had to continue.

'I don't think we can live like this any more, I can't live like this.'

His face collapsed when I said this. 'What am I meant to do? Where can I go? I have no-one.'

It was true: he had no-one but me – of course he had friends, but no-one who loved him as I did.

'I don't know, Piero. That is not my problem. You're going to have to sort yourself out like I'm trying to sort myself out.'

I could see that he was starting to tear up as well. It was the hardest thing I had done in my life up to that point, but I knew I had to do it, for both of us.

'I'm sorry, Piero, I love you. That's why I have to do this.'

'I love you too, Louie.'

We ended there. Neither of us knew what else to say. I left him crying on the street and I walked off down Old Compton Street, crying my eyes out.

I had made my mind up that I could no longer live this way. It ate away at me inside; I couldn't bear the thought of hating this person I loved so much, even though I was no longer in love with him. It was very emotional when we got back to the flat at Goodge Place that day and we both cried a lot. For the first time in a long while we actually hugged each other, I felt that love again that made our relationship so special. I felt I did not want to let go, but my conscience took over my heart. I knew we had reached the end and I had to be really tough.

The flat was in my name, as Piero was still in Italy when I took up the tenancy. I also knew that I couldn't stay there on my own, as there were too many memories of our time together.

After this conversation, I spoke to Carmine and asked if I could stay with him for a while, and of course he said yes. This was when it became very difficult.

Piero had nowhere to go. Even though I knew that I was doing the right thing, I did not want him to be unhappy – but I needed to move on. He eventually found somewhere to stay, in a shared house in Camden. Although things between us were strained for a while and we had no contact for six months, after that time we started to rebuild our relationship as friends. It is still the hardest thing I have ever had to do, because it felt as if I were losing a part of myself.

I DIDN'T feel that I could turn to my family at this point to help me cope with the break-up. Even though everyone knew I was gay, and knew that I was in a relationship, I thought they would not be able to understand it. It felt as if we were living parallel lives and I couldn't cope with family gatherings; I avoided events such as weddings and anniversaries. I felt we had nothing in common beyond the fact that we were family.

I did not want to speak about my life to them: what was I meant to say? I was sure Dad would not be interested in my break-up with Piero. I thought my sisters had enough to deal with on their own; the two eldest each had three children by this point and they had both been divorced by now.

Mum and Dad had problems of their own and I did not think that mine were as important. In their eyes I lived this glamorous life with no responsibilities, and maybe I did not want them to see that it was not all glitz and glamour. I did not want to shatter the illusion that had been created by all the wonderful things I was a part of.

Going home would have forced me to face up to my insecurities and failures, and make me realise my life was no different to theirs at all. When I was in London, I felt as though my life was different: I didn't have to face the realities as there were so many distractions. There were no distractions in Braintree and the last thing I needed was reality slapping me in the face.

I hadn't told Mum and Dad that Piero and I had separated. I couldn't face telling them, especially after a letter I received from Mum, which reminded me how much I was neglecting the family. She pointed out that I had stopped going to family occasions, and since they were aware that I was gay, it was as if I had disowned them. That was not the case at all, but I had become consumed with the love I had for Piero. All of my life I felt as though something were missing and Piero filled that gap. When the relationship started to fail, I knew that my family in Braintree couldn't give me what I needed.

I love my family more than anything in the world, as they do me, but the love they couldn't give me was the one I had found with Piero. I felt more comfortable at this point in my life with my friends; it was Carmine who I felt I could turn to, and who could give me the kind of love I needed. This may sound strange, but I needed to speak to a man about this; I needed to be comforted by someone who understood what I was feeling. There was no-one at home who could offer me this.

In her letter Mum had written that she felt we had drifted apart and had nothing in common; whenever I rang to see how they were, that's all it was, and there was nothing else behind it. I knew she was right, and I felt guilty, but for some reason at this point I wanted to shut them out of my life. I did not want them to be a part of my life; it was mine, and I did not want them to share it, neither the good nor the bad. I had started to experience very bad panic attacks again after the break-up with Piero and I resented my family for it. I did not like being part of this family: I blamed them for our suffering with anxiety and panic attacks, why couldn't we just be like a normal family?

The truth of it is that when I was with them I had to face up to parts of me that I didn't like; I was insecure and frightened, experienced panic attacks and despised myself. The constant battle with myself every day was heightened whenever I was around my family; I felt I was winning the battle if I dealt with these problems on my own. Panic attacks trigger each other in a chain and the longer you can go without one, the better off you will be. I had learned how to deal with it in my own way, in my own environment, and it was without my family.

It made me angry sometimes when I tried to explain to Mum why I didn't want to go to these family occasions. I thought she should understand, of all people, that this was one of the worst things that could happen. I think this is where we are alike: she saw me as being selfish for not wanting to go along, and I saw her as selfish for not understanding. I guess that is why at that time in my life Mum felt that our relationship was drifting, and she was right. Now, don't get upset when you read this, Mum. That was then, and this is now.

Sorry people, I just had to put that in there, because I know what she is like. You see, it's not all razzamatazz: I'm really showing the deep and dark side here. But thank the Lordy for good friends. Carmine was an absolute saviour during this time. The most important thing I had to do was to find somewhere to live. I needed somewhere I felt safe and secure.

WE DECIDED to go on a flat hunt and to have some fun with it. If you have never done this, it's great. When you have nothing to do, it's a great treat to look at properties you have no intention of renting. You can pick up some nice decorating tips.

Everything was so expensive, and I was out of work and of no fixed abode, but a friend suggested I should put my name down for a housing association flat. I sent off the application and received a letter which said I had been accepted, but it might take up to two years. It took a year, almost to the day, to receive the letter saying that they had given me a one-bedroom flat. It is where I still live now.

Even though I said I was only going to stay with Carmine for a couple of weeks, it ended up being a year. As anyone knows who has stayed on a friend's sofa, it becomes tedious after a while. No matter how close you are, it can put a real strain on the relationship.

Carmine and I fell out a couple of times, but never to the point that we were unable to resolve it with a shopping trip to Camden Market. It wasn't like it is now, just shops and modern-day market stalls; you really could get yourself a good bit of vintage at a reasonable price.

I would always go for a shirt – tight-fitting, of course. I've always had fairly prominent breasts. I would say it's hereditary, but it's not at all. Everyone else in the family has false ones, apart from my younger sister Kelly: her tits are her own.

Back to me and my tight shirt: it always started as a complete shirt, but as soon as we got home, I would start by cutting off the cuffs. It then became three-quarter length, short, then sleeveless, collar off, shirt tails off. By this point, it would be ruined and go straight into the bin. But did we ever learn a lesson from it? No.

See, that's how we normally got over our arguments, by laughing at how stupid we were, wasting money we didn't have.

Back to me and my flat – before I moved in, I had a viewing. It was a shithole. Not structurally, although the plaster was falling off some of the walls. The guy who showed me around told me that an old man had died in the flat. I'm usually spooked by things like that, but after a year on the sofa, I would have been happy to see him appear to give me a hand with the decorating.

One good thing that came out of it was that I got a shower. Normally, the Housing Association won't put a shower in, but the old man was disabled. I know this, because his Zimmer frame was in the flat where he had left it, in the shower. At least he went to heaven clean.

I was given the keys a week after viewing the flat, and Carmine and I went into the place and had a cleaning frenzy. Kim and Aggie weren't a patch on us. There wasn't a nook, cranny, or even a fanny that we missed. You really could have eaten your food off the floorboards, because that's all I had – floorboards.

There wasn't a scrap of furniture. Well, I lie – I had one piece of furniture. It was my blue, Gary Barlow sofabed from Habitat. I decided to put that in the bedroom and work my way backwards from the sitting room with the decorating.

The Housing Association was very good and re-lined the walls, where the plaster was falling off. Once that was done, I went straight down to Ikea.

It was a choice between soft furnishings or a laminate floor. After a bit of to-ing and fro-ing, I went for the flooring.

No matter how much I buffed the floorboards in the flat, they weren't going to come up to anything. The flats were also not big on soundproofing. If the neighbour downstairs farted, I heard it. So, the choice was a bit of insulation and laminate flooring all the way through.

It was the first time in my life I felt I had something of my own. Even though I didn't own it, it was much different renting from a housing association to a private landlord. It gave me a sense of security and well-being.

EVEN THOUGH I felt as if I had moved on from Piero, I still wasn't ready for a relationship of any sort. I wasn't interested in just picking someone up and sleeping with them on the first night. The last thing I would want to do is wake up with someone I didn't really know and have to make them tea and toast. I wouldn't have time! I'm a man of routine and habit. It would be too much of a distraction, not being able to go to the gym at my usual time, and having to be concerned about someone I'm not concerned about. I didn't see the point.

The great thing about getting the flat was that I started to see a lot more of my parents. Dad decorated the whole flat for me. I started to help, but after a few strokes of the brush, we decided it would be much easier if I just went shopping with Mum.

This pleased Mum, of course. It reminded me of when I was a kid and the shopping trips I would make with her. I think she missed my support at home, especially when it came to her wardrobe. She wanted to feel like her own person and my sisters would tell her she couldn't go out in whatever she had bought; I would always stick up for her and ask them why not? And when she wasn't in those clothes that my sisters didn't like, *I* certainly was.

I think my love of the low-vee look came from Mum's outfits. Although she never wore hers so low, it was usually a scallop or a cowl neck, so as good as.

Around this time everything seemed to fall into place in my life. Work was very good, and there was always something going on. If it wasn't TOTP or the MTV awards, it would be the Smash Hits awards. Even though I hadn't grown any taller, for some reason I was getting all the gigs.

At these award ceremonies I might be dancing for an artist or employed to dance throughout the show, from the opening through to various acts on the day, such as Madonna, Annie Lennox, or Take That – you get my drift.

It was amazing hanging out backstage with these artists: there was such a buzz. The good thing about working with these people was that you got to hang out directly with them, and that meant we would get AAA passes – Access All Areas. If you didn't, then you would need to start worrying, as that would mean you were outside the circle of the elite working dancers.

If you had been in and then found yourself out, it would be very hard to work your way back. That could happen if you were one of the older dancers, who had run his or her time and had not chosen to get out on their own terms. And that never happened to me: I made the choice to get out while I was still at the top of my game, but I'll tell you about that later.

There is nothing worse than seeing someone dancing behind an artist who could be that artist's mother. I went to Manchester to hook up with a friend of mine who worked for Take That's management. Her name was Ying and we had become friendly on the Take That tour. I went to stay with her for the weekend and she worked for Nigel Martin Smith, Take That's first manager.

When I got to the office, Nigel was there. He asked me if I would be interested in working with a new artist he had. My diary was pretty busy at this time – it was a case of could I fit them in or not? I checked out the dates and I could do them. Some of you may remember the singer Kavanagh. I suppose this was one of the first times I felt as though I was older. I said older, not old: I still had an eight-pack and an ass like a peach.

When I went to the first day of rehearsals, bless him, Kavanagh was cute as a button but he looked about 12. Well, a job was a job, was a job. Because he was a new artist, we had to do every road show: when the radio stations would go to every town near you. That's where I was: at a town near you, and back again. After doing that in the day, we would normally drive across the country to some under-18s club because at that time Kavanagh wasn't old enough to get into most clubs.

One thing that always amazed me was why they couldn't book a club in the town where the radio show had taken place. We always had to travel across the country to do the night show. These jobs were hard, and you would just hope that the artist would make it; if they did, you knew that you would be in for loads of work. Kavanagh didn't do badly, but he definitely wasn't doing as well as a girl group that had arrived on the scene while we were on tour.

There were many radio shows that we would arrive at only to see this group there ahead of us. They just became bigger and bigger, and I decided this was who I wanted to be working for. And so did everyone else.

15

I'll Tell You What I Want

Have you guessed yet? Aaaah, colours of the world! Spice up your life! Yes, the Spice Girls. We weren't on speaking terms by any means, but we were nodding. In all the time I had been dancing and been around pop stars, I had never seen anything like the buzz around them.

They were literally rushed on stage with loads of security, and then rushed off. They were rushed in and out so quickly that even the nodding stopped.

There were rumours that they were going to do 'An Audience With' and they were looking for a lot of dancers. At the time, we didn't know if it was true or just Chinese whispers, but the word on the dance vine was that if you were used as a main dancer on the 'Audience' show, then there was a good chance that you would do their world tour.

I was booked almost every day working with Kavanagh, and I loved working with him because he was so sweet and funny. But the thought of missing out on the chance to dance with the Spice Girls because I was booked at an under-18s club did not make me happy. Honestly, it got beyond a joke. There were rumours that the dancers had been cast and some dancers even tried to put others off auditioning by saying they already had the job. Well, stop the press, it was true. The Spice Girls were doing 'An Audience With' and on the day of the audition in London, where was I? Of course, I was up North at some shitty under-18s club.

What I should have done is pull a sicky, but I thought I would go down the professional route and ask if there was any chance I could miss that day's show so that I could audition for the Spice Girls.

Wrong choice – the answer was no, and I was so pissed off. Normally it wouldn't bother me too much if I had to miss an audition but if the rumour was true, and you could become one of their tour dancers, that was different. Everyone knew how big this tour would be: these girls were massive.

On the day of the audition I slipped into an almost suicidal depression. I gave a crap performance that night. I couldn't even push out a split, and that's something I can normally slip into at the drop of a hat. But these legs weren't for splitting.

My one saving grace was that Carmine was at the audition and I just couldn't wait to get off the stage to find out what had happened, and who had got the job. Was it true about the tour? If it was, then Kavanagh's career was about to be cut very short.

Everyone who I thought would get the job actually got the job, including Carmine. I was so pleased for him. There was never any kind of competition between us. I found it really hard to express my feelings of joy for him, though. But there was a glimmer of light for me at the end of the tunnel.

The Spice Girls had their main corps of dancers, but they would also have some extras. I mean, extras! I thought I had left all that behind me. But sometimes, where there is a small opening, you just have to make a big hole. Being the wonderful friend Carmine was, he had a word with the choreographer, who knew me. She said I didn't have to audition and that I could be one of the extras.

I had asked him to ask if I could be one of the main dancers, even though I wasn't at the audition, but one of the dates clashed with Kavanagh, who at this point was unconscious. I had slightly suffocated him with my jockstrap while on the phone to Carmine.

THE DAY of the 'Audience With' show had arrived and the main dancers were on stage with the Spice Girls, all chatty and pally, while I was almost outside the studio, on the last step next to the fire exit.

There was a moment when Emma looked over, and I gave the nod that I always gave on tour with Kavanagh, but I got no reaction. As I mentioned before, main dancers were VVIP, but extras almost did not exist. While the main dancers went off with the girls, the extras went into a Green Room, where you would be lucky if you got a custard cream and a cup of tea. Carmine, in the meantime, was putting in an order with Spice Girls' security for his choice of pizza!

I remember thinking, 'I just can't believe it'. I knew I had been lucky and done some wonderful jobs, but the thought

of missing out on going on tour with the Spice Girls, if the rumour was true about the main dancers, was making me eat my own spine.

While I was eating my own insides with envy, someone opened the door to our dressing room/Green Room/anyone's room. It was the choreographer's assistant, who called out my name. I felt like I was being saved. A moment earlier, it had been grey clouds and thunderstorms, with lightning striking my heart, but she was like a ray of sunshine.

Without an ounce of coolness or dignity, I trampled over man, woman and child to get to her, in case it was Louise she was calling for. Once again, thank God for having someone on the inside – Carmine. As they say in the business, it's not what you know, it's *who* you know.

She explained that they wanted someone to do acrobatics in one of the numbers and flip across the stage. It would have to be choreographed within one of the main numbers. I felt the gates were opening to me, and she was my St Peter.

This was my chance, this could be my ticket to Spice World. I was taken back into the main studio, which was empty except for the Spice Girls, five dancers, four security, one choreographer, her assistant, and – yes – *me*!

I felt like bursting into 'Rose's Turn', from *Gypsy*. (I know she is having a nervous breakdown in the song, but I had been close to one all day.)

As I walked down the stairs towards them all, I didn't bother giving the nod, as it no longer seemed to get a reaction. Well, lo and behold, Emma turned around, looked at me and said, 'Hello, how are you? Are you still dancing with Kavanagh?' So did Geri, then Mel, and Mel, then VB.

Now I felt at home. I knew once I had done my flips and

an open layout summersault, not only would they remember me as a dancer with Kavanagh, they would remember my name. Fame! I'm gonna live forever. (Sorry, I had to put that bit in – I couldn't resist.)

We rehearsed the number, and my backflips and open layout summersault were spectacular, if I do say so myself, considering I had as much room as a postage stamp to do them on.

After the rehearsal I got what you might call an upgrade, to the male dancers' dressing room. I was no longer in some generic piece of tat from the TV department's wardrobe, I was now in the Spice Camp, with stylists and hair and make-up.

Costume, check. Hair, check. Make-up, check. The show began, and it finished with rapturous applause. My performance was successful – not that they showed any of it. When I got back home and watched it, while I was flipping they were showing the audience. That didn't bother me in the slightest. The fact was that I felt one step closer to the chance of being a Spice Boy, whereas a week earlier, I could have been charged with murder by jockstrap of a young, up-and-coming pop star.

I suppose it might be true what they say: if you want something enough and put it out there, the universe will answer your call. In saying that, it could all be a pile of crap, because the universe didn't answer my call – it was Carmine.

16

Spice Boy

EVERY MALE dancer was waiting to hear when the auditions for the Spice Girls' world tour would take place but in the end, there was no audition because the girls were too busy. It was down to the choreographer, Priscilla, to choose the dancers. As you can imagine, she was one hell of a popular person in the dance world. One thing I knew about Priscilla, was that she wouldn't choose dancers because she fancied them or because they were cute. Obviously looks played a part, but it would only get you so far when it came to performance at that level.

I know I proved my worth at the 'Audience' show, and I know the reason she didn't pick me as a main dancer was because I couldn't make the initial audition and one of the rehearsal dates. But what I also knew, once again through the dance vine, was that she was looking for versatile dancers, and that was certainly me.

Believe it or not, there were not that many of us around – versatile, that is. There was Carmine, and really, I can't think of anyone else. I could do tap, gymnastics and acrobatics (there *is* a difference). Lyrical jazz, contemporary, hip hop, a bit of Latin, and very basic ballroom (I think I'm getting my point across about the versatility). Carmine was the same, but without the backflips. I knew I was in the running, as did Carmine, and about 20 other dancers. Every day in class, we were constantly asking, 'Have you heard anything?' You only got the call if you had been chosen, so if someone hadn't received the call, it meant bad news for you.

This went on for about four weeks. Every time the phone rang and I didn't recognise the number, I thought I was going to give birth – not only when my phone rang, but when any of the boys received a call. Pineapple would go silent and everyone pretended they weren't listening in, but they were. It got to the point where I was begging for an epidural – and then it happened. No, don't be stupid, I didn't give birth: Carmine got the call. He could have been a dartboard, the number of daggers that focussed on him when he told us that he had got the job. Of course, after the daggers came the congratulations dripping with venom.

It was obvious that the calls were being made now, as only five minutes had passed between Carmine and Christian receiving their calls. Eventually half an hour passed and I became more agitated. They were on the phone only two minutes to Carmine – how long could it take to call seven people?

By this time, Carmine and I had left Pineapple and were at Old Compton Street, having a latte – full-fat milk and chocolate. Those were the days! I was checking my phone every 30 seconds to make sure I was in reception and I hadn't missed a call. I was, and I hadn't. Suddenly my phone rang and there it was – Private Number.

You know those moments you wait such a long time for that when they eventually arrive, you don't want to deal with them? Well, this wasn't one of them. I was ready for it. There was still that slight worry that maybe this time they were going to tell people they hadn't got the job. What was I thinking? Of course they wouldn't. This was definitely a 'yes'. Wasn't it?

The person on the other end of the line introduced himself as the tour manager for the Spice Girls and told me that I had been chosen as a dancer for the world tour. He said he would be in touch towards the end of the week with further details. It was short and sweet, but that was all I needed to hear. As you can imagine, after I put the phone down, the first thing Carmine and I thought was, 'Shit, what are we going to wear on tour for a year?' This meant a whole new wardrobe.

Really, we were a bit premature, considering we hadn't signed a contract, or knew how much we would be earning each week. But when a boy has to shop, he has to shop! And that's exactly what we did. We shopped 'til we dropped.

My family was very excited that I would be going on tour with the Spice Girls – not surprising, considering how huge they were. There were constant requests for autographs for friends, and friends of friends, and requests for tickets to the shows. I suspected these friends of friends were trying to make money by selling the tickets on, as the shows themselves were sold out.

REHEARSALS STARTED a week and a half after we got the phone call – time enough to do serious damage to our credit cards. It was fate obviously, or we would not have had the time to get our shopping fix.

We received our rehearsal itinerary and the first thing we noticed was that we would not be rehearsing in London, as we had assumed. Rehearsals would take place in Dublin for just over a month and before I knew it, I was checking in to our hotel, which was actually about half an hour outside the city. The Spice Girls had arrived a week early to start their rehearsals and they were staying in apartments on a golf course, about 10 minutes away from our hotel.

The hotel was an old country house that had been converted and I could tell from that point on that it would be a good tour. They did not put us up in some dodgy dive above a pub: each one of us had a large double room, with enough room for a sofa and a few pirouettes. My room even had a four-poster bed!

We arrived the day before rehearsals were due to begin, and we were all very excited: we had entered the Spice Bubble. When we arrived at the hotel, we did not have to check in – there was someone there to check *us* in. There was someone there to check our bags and make sure they got to the right room; there was someone we could contact about anything we might need. From that moment on, we did not have to think any more. All we had to do was learn the choreography and dance. Other people took care of our well-being – our food, washing, etc.

You may wonder why some pop stars seem out of touch with reality. If that was how we were being treated as dancers, you only have to imagine how these artists are pampered.

STILL GOT IT, NEVER LOST IT!

I never saw any of the Spice Girls having a diva tantrum or being demanding, and that's what makes the job one of the best I have ever had. We were never made to feel separate from the artists: they involved us in their lives and were on our level.

Rehearsals started at 10 the following morning, and I was ready and packed at 9.30. It felt like my first day at school. Our People Carrier arrived to take us to rehearsals, with blacked-out windows, of course. It took 10 minutes to travel the winding roads to get to the golf course where the girls were staying, and where we would be rehearsing (I knew it was posh because the grass was like velvet). We continued down the drive for what seemed like a mile until we arrived at the main building. Even though I had seen the Spice Girls many times when I was on tour with Kavanagh, and got a little close to them when I performed on their 'Audience With' show, I still felt nervous and excited about going to meet them, knowing that we would be together for the next year.

When we entered the studio, the girls were halfway through rehearsing a number, which they didn't finish. Instead they came straight over to us with boundless energy, especially Mel B. They greeted us with hugs and kisses, which was great because they put us at ease straightaway. Then that was it – we went straight into rehearsals. The girls had already learned about five or six numbers, and we just had to fit in. As we started to learn the choreography, the girls sat at the front of the studios watching us, laughing and giggling. Mel B was very funny, and in her Leeds accent she said to Jimmy, whom she later married, 'Are you gay?'

He replied 'No', and her response was 'Go on!' as if she had just scored one for the team. It was not that she singled him out – she went along the line. When she got to me, I said to her, 'Do you really need to ask?' and she agreed she didn't in my case.

After a day of rehearsals the girls invited us back to one of their apartments to chill out and have some drinks. That's how we ended almost every night after rehearsals, when the girls were there. As well as rehearsing they were flying here, there and everywhere, doing one-off shows. That's why they had started rehearsals a week before us. It was amazing – I couldn't believe how hard they worked. Even though they had people doing everything for them, it was exhausting watching them sometimes. I think that's why they enjoyed our company, because they didn't have to be 'on': they could just chill and relax.

WE HUNG out mainly with Emma, Mel B and Geri. I think Victoria might have been on the phone to David, while Mel C was so disciplined and professional, she knew she would be paying for it the next day. Seeing their schedule, I think that if I had been a Spice Girl, I would have been just like her. Mel B was mouthy and mad, and said whatever she thought, which used to make me piss my pants. Geri could be a bit hot and cold, but my favourite by far was, and still is, Emma.

We just seemed to bond and there were many similarities between us in our upbringing. We both came from loving families and had a love of the same foods, especially beans on toast, and tuna and mayonnaise on white bread – none of that brown crap. We also loved a good cocktail sausage, and a party wouldn't be a party without a bit of pineapple and cheese on a stick.

Before we knew it, our month of rehearsals in Ireland was over and we were making our way to Zurich for the first show. Even though we were well rehearsed, I still did not feel ready, but I don't think you do on the first night of any show.

We got to the venue in the morning for rehearsals but the girls were not there. I don't think they were even in the country – they were doing something somewhere else. They never seemed to have a moment to themselves. The stage was amazing: it was massive, with three different levels, a central staircase and a lot of sparkle. You would not believe the number of people working to set up the stage – crew, electricians, lighting – there were literally hundreds of them. The riggers wore harnesses and usually had a tattoo or two. They put in the lighting, clambering all over the set like little monkeys on their wires.

Once we had finished rehearsing and everyone was happy with their bits and bobs, we would go to catering, which travelled with us. Yes, a whole kitchen. It is amazing to think they just set up shop wherever we were. The food was great and there was always a varied menu to choose from. Once dinner was done, that was it – we knew showtime was closer. We went back to our dressing rooms to check our costumes, which the wardrobe department would have put on a rail with our names. The costumes were placed in the order in which they would be used during the show.

I always checked the quick-change rail – to make sure that all the costumes I needed would be there when I couldn't get back to the dressing room to change. At the end of the day, it is always best to check for yourself and then you can't blame anyone else. I have seen it too many times, when someone has come off stage for a quick change, only to find their costume missing.

After that it was hair, make-up, costume and showtime! The first show is always hard – you have to think about everything you are doing. Once you get into the run, it gets easier – it becomes like muscle memory. Your body remembers the movements and you can relax into the performance.

One of the most exciting moments of the first night is always just before the music starts, while the lights are still up at the front. You can hear a sea of voices laughing and shouting, but as soon as the lights go down the whole place erupts into one massive scream. When the music kicks in, the screams become 10 times louder and at this point it feels like your stomach is on a fast spin. This is when your muscle memory comes in useful, because your mind goes completely blank as you try to remember every step.

Just as I am about to go on stage I feel as if I'm going to explode. Quite frankly, I do – on to the stage. There is no other feeling like it, when you are dancing in front of 15 or 20,000 people – it feels right where you belong. Even though you know they are not screaming directly for you, you cannot help but get caught up in the excitement when you are performing.

Then suddenly, in a flash, the show is over – the first night is over, and I am already looking forward to the next venue. There is so much adrenaline that you feel as if you could do another show. But usually we go straight to the dressing rooms, shower, and then get on to the tour bus.

These are amazing – they have everything, including bedrooms, living rooms and kitchens. They are like a hotel on wheels, with air conditioning and TV screens in your beds.

We would put in an order for food and when we arrived, it would be waiting – whatever we wanted. As you can imagine, it got pretty raucous on the bus – five straight boys and two gays. While they were chatting about the girls in the audience, I would be on tidy duties, spraying and wiping surfaces, fluffing cushions and generally prancing around.

The shows normally finished around 10.30 pm, but by the time we finished showers and got on the bus it was usually 11.30 when we were all on board. I was always ready in half an hour flat, while Jimmy Gulzar was always late. I didn't mind tidy duties, but I couldn't bear lateness. That's when my testosterone would kick in. Jimmy and I had a few run-ins, including one spectacular altercation in the showers – not the kind you are thinking.

Living on top of each other for a year, it was inevitable that we would flip out occasionally. I'm surprised we took these arguments seriously, him standing there naked and me in a micro mini-towel. In saying that, I had arguments as a pussy, with whiskers and wearing another tail, with a mouse in tap shoes. I suppose that could top it, couldn't it?

It really was one of the best experiences of my life and it was rare that we would have any kind of argument. Sometimes Mel B and Emma would join us on the tour bus. I think they just wanted to slum it and have a rest from the private jet. I suppose that happens – you get so used to one thing that it no longer seems glamorous. I mean, I always get a cab now instead of taking a bike taxi. Occasionally I go back to one – it's a nice view from behind one of those South American riders. I mean the view over Waterloo Bridge, of course.

On one occasion Mel B and Emma joined us on the bus from Lausanne to Paris. Emma had asked her mum to buy us all M&S pyjamas, blue and white stripes. We had to stop for refuelling at a service station and we all decided to go shopping for nibbles in our new M&S PJs. With seven dancers and two Spice Girls, we weren't going to just fall off the bus – it was choreographed with military precision. I think we looked like we had escaped from an institution, standing there at night in our stripey blue and white pyjamas. The girls were recognised instantly, but we were all having so much fun that they didn't care. I think it just felt nice for them, to do something normal – you know what I mean.

Another time they travelled with us, we had to sleep on the tour bus until check-in. The girls were late as they should have arrived the day before on their jet, so their rooms were ready. Emma and I had become very friendly by this time on the tour, and instead of sleeping on the bus for another five hours or so, I checked into her room with her. And by room, I mean suite.

We nearly always stayed in the same hotels as the girls, which were always very nice. There was the odd one or two – in Munich, I think. Each room had a theme, which all seemed to be Seventies porn. My bathroom had a glass floor over sand, seashells and starfish. So I had the boys in quick for a jaccuzi, and we ended up photographing our rears. While at this hotel Emma and I went shopping, which we did in every city. When we got back to the hotel this time, Emma was frightened by a man coming towards us wearing a half veil and she ran off screaming. I took off after her and later found out that we had run away from Michael Jackson.

WE HAD more cities to get to and more shopping discounts to claim, so we weren't too bothered. Italy was always good for shopping, and in Bologne we had a special time. Carmine and I tagged along with the girls on this particular shopping trip, and when we were in Dolce & Gabbana the staff were all over the girls like a rash. They couldn't get enough in their baskets, and while it wasn't all free, they had a great discount.

Of course Carmine and I asked if we could slip a few items into their baskets, which they agreed, so we filled up one or two. I don't know who ended up paying – they never asked, and we never offered – so thank you again! It's not as if we were looking for freebies, but with such a busy schedule it was that easy to slip our minds!

When we were travelling we would do evenings out, as well as day trips. We never knew who we would bump into on our evenings out. My cut-off shirts from Camden were not going to suffice in the capitals of Europe, so I was grate-ful for that trip to Dolce & Gabbana.

Whenever we left a hotel it was a mission each time getting past the army of paparazzi and fans. We dancers found it exciting, but I don't think the girls really did; there was usually a convoy of Mercedes vans with blacked-out windows.

In Paris we went via the convoy to an amazing restaurant and on to a club – I don't remember the names, after so many years on the road, and so many venues. There were a lot of

French celebrities at the club, but we didn't have a clue who they were. It was a small place, with red sofas and walls, and the guest DJ was LL Cool J. He was knocking out some great tunes and we were all having a good time. All except Emma, bless her: for some reason she started crying in the middle of the club. She had been drinking Bacardi, which made her cry, then laugh, then cry – it was a great evening, spent crying with laughter.

We had so many nights like this in Europe, in beautiful restaurants, and with VVIPs in clubs, and I was also Emma's date for any premieres or parties she attended. Carmine and I accompanied her to one such premiere in Amsterdam and she looked stunning in a baby blue silk mini-dress, with a faux-mink crop jacket (which I had my eye on), and some Prada wedges. I remember the shoes because they weren't the buffalo boots, which I hated. There is nothing feminine about those, is there, ladies? I mean, really.

Emma has the most amazing shoe collection, which I'd like to put down to my influence. I guess we all make mistakes with footwear when we're young, so it's more likely due to experience.

I think one of the reasons she and I became so close on tour was that neither of us had a partner at that time. Victoria had David, Mel B had Jimmy, Geri was going out with another of the dancers, Christian, and Mel C was married to her dedication to the gym, which left Emma for me.

AFTER EUROPE we had a month off before heading to America. The dancers might have had time off, but the girls did not stop working. I spoke to Emma almost every day for that month; we had become so used to each other's company after four months on the road, we were like family.

It was horrible coming back to reality for that month, and life outside the tour was less fun. Suddenly I had to cook for myself and do my own washing – I couldn't wait to get back in the bubble.

We flew to Miami at the end of the month off to begin the tour. I was looking forward to this, as I had never been there. But I didn't get to see much of it, and I was disappointed that it didn't look anything like *Miami Vice* – no sign of Don Johnson anywhere.

The tour buses were a world apart from the ones we had in Europe – it was like travelling in a posh hotel suite, and even had a bidet, which we used for washing our feet. What else are they for? Nibbles on these buses were a different game altogether and a packet of crisps could last a week. Luckily the weather was hot, which meant that we sweated throughout each show. The meals were so supersize, we would have ended up supersize ourselves! It's just unnecessary, isn't it?

Fans in America were supersize in their eagerness: we were used to the European fans being dedicated, but this was unexpected. When we were in Europe we would play to 20- or 30,000 people, but in America it was suddenly 70- or 90,000 people, in football stadiums.

The magnitude of the stars we got to meet was also much higher in America. At Madison Square Garden we knew that

Madonna would be watching the show, but we didn't know if we would get to meet her. When we got to the venue, Emma told me Madonna was expected backstage to meet the girls. So before the show I could be found hanging out casually by the girls' changing room like some stalker fan, just so I could get a glimpse of her.

I heard on the walkie-talkies that Madonna was on her way and I thought I'd get to say hello, but all I saw when the doors opened was four bouncers the size of houses. In the middle of this housing estate of flesh I caught a glimpse of feet and hair, but I got my moment when she came out afterwards with the girls and Emma introduced me to her. I got to shake her hand and I remember thinking how tiny she was, and how someone so small could be such a phenomenon. I was surprised at how normal she seemed, but there was something inexplicable, beyond all that. She was Madonna! Small, unassuming, born to perform – it's like we were separated at birth.

We also met Tracey Ullman, who went to Italia Conti before I did. She was already very popular in America with the *Tracey Ullman Show* and I felt she really enjoyed her time with us. She has a very English sense of humour and I got a different feeling from her, compared to Madonna. I could have easily spent the whole day with her and felt we were on the same level – I've always found it's easier to be with funny people.

We stayed at the Four Seasons in Beverly Hills for two weeks while we did shows in Orange County. Jon Bon Jovi was staying at the hotel at the same time and I would see him in the gym in the morning. He is very handsome in real life, with an amazing body.

STILL GOT IT, NEVER LOST IT!

In Phoenix, Arizona, the Hoffmaster, David Hasselhoff was staying in our hotel. He was very nice and made a point of coming to say hello to us all. We met a lot of chat show hosts, and other celebrities who the girls knew, because they had been on their shows. We went out in New York and LA, as well as Minneapolis, in trilby hats in tribute to Prince. But we didn't go out as much as we did in Europe and spent more time with each other at the various hotels. We were advised not to go out in many other cities and states because of their negative attitudes to gays.

Some people we met didn't know where England was and had no knowledge of countries outside America. I didn't want to be the one to burst their bubble and introduce them to the realities of the real world. It was like travelling back in time in some areas, not just because of attitudes towards sexuality but race as well. This alone put us off going out altogether in some places.

The last show we did in Texas, the security warned us about going out because I was gay. It was shocking that such a big state could be so homophobic – or so I was told. I didn't go out, so I didn't experience it: I could only rely on what I was told. But in 1998, I expected a bit more. However, we had our own world in the Spice Bubble and we didn't need others to enter it – we had each other.

WE TOURED Europe and North America, including Canada, for almost a year. Unfortunately, we didn't get to meet Celine Dion – she might have been in LA then. This will make me sound stupid, but I was surprised that it

Me giving smoky eyes, while Emma is on fire;
looking hot, hot, hot!

was nothing like America. The Canadians soon set me
straight – it was nothing like America, because it was Canada!
The Canadians we met were much more open and relaxed.

You would think that a gay man travelling the world
would take the opportunity to taste the fruits it had to offer,

but I'm not that type of person. It didn't feel necessary, and there was so much going on in the bubble that there was little desire on my part.

One evening Carmine and the girls persuaded me to chat up the waiter in a restaurant in Canada. He was giving me the eye and I invited him back to my hotel room. I had already decided that when I got back to the hotel, I wouldn't answer the door – I had gone off the idea.

An hour later, he knocked on the door and I was very cool with him. It was different being out with the crowd and I closed down. Meanwhile, he drank the mini-bar dry, and I was definitely not rising to the occasion: the last thing I wanted was a drunk in my hotel room. I find drunk people annoying when they have gone past their limit, but when you don't know them, it gets a bit much. I got very frosty and sent him on his way, then knocked on Carmine's door. His room was next to mine and he opened the door expecting lots of gossip, but all he got was a good laugh at me and called me a frigid old freak. Which I was, I suppose, frigid – he could have gone a bit easy on the freak.

I didn't bother doing that again – I didn't need to. I could go and sleep with Emma if I wanted a kiss and a cuddle.

Our time in America went very quickly and was coming to a rapid end. The thought of facing reality again was a nightmare. Yet, even though it was glamorous and exciting, there were moments when I wished for my own bed.

We were all looking forward to the return to the UK because the girls would be playing Wembley Stadium. On the day of the show at Wembley, Emma asked me to go with her to her car. I was expecting some nice juicy gossip that no-one else could hear: I knew she had a little love interest of her own by this time, which I discovered in Manchester. That's where I met Jade and I remember telling him he had better treat her right. We laugh about it now, but he obviously took note. He was cute as a button, too.

Instead she gave me a present, as a thank you for the last few months on tour. We had become such good friends and told each other everything. When I opened the present, I found a beautiful Rolex watch. I was beside myself, that she had taken the time to think about me and to choose a gift: the girls did not have a minute to themselves and I was very moved that she had gone to so much effort. We had already been around the world together and had some incredible experiences and I love her dearly.

As you can imagine, the last show was really emotional for everyone. We were a big family of crew, dressers, cooks, make-up artists. The sad thing is that when these jobs finish, you don't keep in contact with most of these lovely people. Occasionally you bump into people on other jobs, but for the most part you go your own ways. I am lucky that Emma remains a true friend.

As a dancer it is difficult to save money – you never know when the next job is going to come. The idea of having to return to reality and look for work was daunting, but we were lucky that we had some money from the tour. All our expenses had been paid for, so we were able to save. I did not have to rush to find work, but I was also aware that I didn't have the luxury of time.

17

Cats

Once again, I discovered that it's not what you know, it's *who* you know. While I had been away for a year doing the Spice Girls' tour, a friend of mine, Jason Gardiner (the Ice Queen as some of you may know him, from *Dancing on Ice*), had been working in *Cats* at the New London Theatre in the West End. A West End contract is normally a year, unless you are a star performer. Jason was coming up to the end of his contract and the producers were recasting for the show. The resident choreographer, Chrissie Cartwright, asked Jason if he could recommend anyone for the role of Mr Mistoffeles.

This is a big dance role in *Cats*, and is normally performed by classical dancers, which reflects the choreography. His name is Magical Mr Mistoffeles, so the dancer needs to be able to do amazing tricks as well as the classical movements. Jason recommended me to Chrissie and she asked to see me. This was a role that I always wanted to do, but because it required singing I wasn't confident that I would ever get it, and I had never auditioned for it.

I met Jason on his first week in London from Australia. He was in my place in class, centre front, at Pineapple. To put yourself centre front in a class takes a lot of guts – even in Italy, the diva in class had not dared put herself centre front. I went up to him to make him aware that he was in my place in class. I think he said something along the lines of, 'Well, it's not your place now.' I remember thinking, 'You vile Australian bitch, you had better be good.'

As it happens, he was very good. It worked out to be a class of all classes – it was a battle to the death. I didn't want anyone coming in to class, taking my place centre front and taking my glory. What a class it was – everyone knew we were battling with each other. If he did a kick, I went higher; if he did a turn, I went faster. It was a battle to the end, our legs like dead weights. We didn't speak throughout this, it was an unacknowledged battle, and we both think we won that day.

After class I was walking home towards Goodge Street when I noticed him behind me. That's all he was to me at that time, a nameless 'him' (bitch). I kept looking back with venom, expecting him to turn off, but he was still behind me. I thought he was following me and that he had some balls to be doing all of this in one day. Eventually I stopped and asked him if he *was* following me. In his broad Australian accent, he told me he lived just one street down from me and we started laughing about what had happened in class that day. Since then, we have remained friends.

If any of you wonder if Jason is the real deal and has big balls, he certainly is and does. What you see is what you get. There is also a very sensitive and caring side to Mr Gardiner and he is incredibly funny with it. Most people don't get to see this side of him, but we've had many nights together when we've had to get the Tena Lady out to soak up the odd dribble.

It must show when you audition for a role that you are not desperate for it. I had just come back from one of the biggest tours that any dancer would have given anything to do, so I was relaxed in my audition. I knew it wouldn't bother me if I didn't get the role, but I wanted to do my best. After so many months on tour, I was technically loose because we hadn't been doing classes. I would have needed a few months to get back on top form, but I did not have the time.

A week after he asked me, I went in to meet the panel. I had not been in that position for a year, with the hunger in the audition among the dancers: I had felt so safe for the last year that this experience sparked the fire of competition again in me. Now I started looking at the dancers and my adrenaline kicked in. Suddenly I was hungry for the role and wanted to get on the stage to show them what I could do.

I COULDN'T believe how excited I was to be on stage auditioning for *Cats*. I first heard the music at Notley High School, age 12, and danced around to the Jellicle Ball, not knowing what I was doing.

There I was, being given the correct choreography, on the actual stage – this seemed the culmination of everything I had worked for. When the music started, I knew the job had to be mine – there was no other audition or job that I had gone for which felt so right. This was what dancing was about. I had never wanted to be a classical dancer: I was too short for anything but token roles and I found some of the classical pieces boring. The role of Mr Mistoffeles in *Cats* was a modern ballet role, a marriage of magic and dance, with classical moves mixed with lyrical jazz. The moment the music started, I was in heaven – I would love to go back and do it again.

With all of this emotion inside me, mixed with a nonchalance about getting the role, the numbers were reduced until we were down to five. The recalls began, the part of the audition process I didn't like – you are close but have to struggle through. I decided I had to fight, fight, fight for this love, aka Cheryl Cole.

I knew the role was made for me and I was confident about my dancing in the audition; I also knew it was my singing that would let me down, and it did. I tried, but I was not up to the standard needed for a solo role in a West End show – and I knew it.

We were three dancers left and I was the last to go in. At least in this situation, they tell you personally whether or not you have got the role. I had not seen the other two dancers who went before me leave, because you left by a different exit after your audition. Even though I knew I had danced all nine lives out of the role in the audition, I was prepared to hear that I had not got the role. I just needed to know that my dancing was good enough, and that it was my singing that had let me down.

You have to go on stage and see the outline of the panel in the auditorium, with the voices coming out of the dark. It was as I had expected. The musical director was a lovely man, Dan Bolin. He tried very hard with my singing – I knew he really liked me, but my best wasn't good enough. He was very sweet, but told me what I knew: that my singing was not of the standard required for the role. That confirmed what I knew, and I only wanted to hear from Chrissie Cartwright that my dancing had been fine.

She said it was a shame that my singing had not been good enough, but that I had danced beautifully, with spectacular tricks. I had created magic with the choreography and she would like to offer me the part.

I was nodding my head in agreement, but had not registered that she was offering me the part. It was only when I heard her say 'Congratulations' that I wondered why she was saying it – then I pieced together what had gone before. I had a cheeky moment, when I punched the air and did the pull in fist, and said, 'Yes!'

I REALLY could not believe it: I felt extremely lucky, and also very proud of myself. I knew this was going to be a real challenge, but I couldn't wait to start. I did not have to wait that long, as rehearsals were going to start a week later.

That's when my insecurities kicked in – would I be good enough? What would people think of me? But these are all part of a dancer's life.

It's amazing how quickly a dancer's body can kick back into action. It's as I said before, muscle memory. I didn't remember it being so painful, but I got back on my legs quickly. 'On your legs' is a dancer's term, which means that when you execute a move, you don't find yourself wobbling.

Ninety-five per cent of *Cats* is dancing and every rehearsal was like an eight-hour class. The Jellicle Ball alone is 20 minutes long; some of the cats were in all of it, others only parts of the ball. I was in pretty much all of it, and it took time to get used to a 20-minute dance number. Once I got used to it, it felt fabulous, and my body looked amazing. I lost about half a stone, and there wasn't much to lose to start with, and I was ripped – but I had to be, in Lycra from head to foot. Luckily my costume was black so I could afford an extra inch or two, if I needed it.

The white cat had her work cut out there, though. It was a desired role for the girls, but it must have been a battle at the best of times. Can you imagine having to wear white Lycra from head to foot for a year?

I got to love my Lycra – I would even crawl around in it at home, but I hated wearing the yak-hair wig. I don't know if it was made from Yak's hair, but it felt like it was. It got very hot after two hours of dancing and my head would feel like a kettle at full boil.

It meant a lot when you finally got your Lycra and your wig – even though I hated the wig – but getting your tail was the highest achievement. It meant you were a full pussy – it was like a coronation.

Chrissie Cartwright was really into her job and very dedicated, so much so that I really do believe she thought we were cats. We built up relationships with other pussies on stage, and the white cat and I got on rather well. We would sniff each other's tails, not for fun but because this is what we had learned in pussy school. We had to nuzzle each other while sniffing, and learn how to spray our turf – basically, to do as pussies do.

Now, I never did, but some of the Tom cats would get a bit excited – all that rubbing up and down in Lycra. It wasn't

Me being Magical Mr Mistoffelees.

a wise thing to do, getting so worked up that you had everything on show. But if you have ever rubbed up against anyone in Lycra, you will know that it's quite a sensational sensation. My spit guard was up for that last bit.

I had an amazing time in *Cats* for the first six months. It was the most rewarding physical work I had ever done, but also the most demanding. I loved the Jellicle Ball in the first half and my main piece in the second half. My number was 'Magical Mr Mistoffeles', which was sung by all of the cast to me and then I would do my big number.

I arrived on stage wearing a velvet jacket with shoulder pads that would have put Krystle Carrington to shame, with flashing lights that you would find on a Christmas tree. All this while descending on to the stage via a long rope. It was a truly magical number that always received a standing ovation and rapturous applause, whoever performed it. I was told that mine was one of the most spectacular Mr Mistoffeles; not necessarily one of the most precise on the classical moves, but I pulled all the tricks out of the bag – back flips, summersaults, free hand cartwheels, twisting walkovers and chest rolls, to name a few.

There is no feeling like knowing you have done a good job because of the audience reaction. It is possible for a dancer to go through the motions, but I put my heart and soul into every performance and it gives the audience a special feeling when they can see that dedication.

AFTER THE first six months I started to give my heart to something else, which was one of the biggest mistakes of my life. I had not seen anyone since Piero, nothing beyond drinks or dinner with a few guys. Six months into *Cats* I met a guy at a club who, for some reason, I couldn't stop thinking about. There wasn't anything particularly special about him, I think maybe he was quite charming – I'm not sure what the attraction was. Professionally, I felt fulfilled and everything was going well, so the timing was right for me to feel that I could be in a relationship of sorts. I wasn't expecting to get into a relationship, but somehow I found myself in one.

I thought it was love – I had not had a partner for a long time and it took over my life. My performances in *Cats* suffered as a result. All I wanted to do was spend time with him and while I was at work, I was preoccupied with what he was doing. I felt insecure and out of control, and although I did not want to compare it to what had happened with Piero years before, I lost faith in everyone.

I wanted it to work, I wanted to invest time in the relationship; this included my career, but it felt like he was just taking, the more I gave. It was not his fault, I was desperate to love. I had not loved anyone for four or five years and I had so much to give. Maybe it was too much for him: I was very generous with my time and friends, and he enjoyed that aspect of my lifestyle. I wondered whether he was with me more for my friends than because he felt anything special for me.

I would take sick days, just so I could be at home with him, even though he would spend his time on the computer and not pay much attention to me. It seems the case that wherever there is something good, something bad is always lurking around the corner. I was neglecting the best thing to have happened to me in my professional life for the sake of an obsession with someone. It was not love, which normally fits in with your life. I regret neglecting my work, which gave me so much more pleasure than that relationship ever could.

My biggest regret is that after my year's contract on *Cats* was up, they did not ask me to renew. It was not unheard of for them to ask someone to sign on again if they were good. I knew how much I had taken the piss by taking time off: I had made it clear that I didn't care about the job any more and I regret that most. Not only had I let the show down, but I had let myself down as well. People often say there is a lesson in every experience, but this is a lesson I should have learned years before in Italy when I was with Piero.

18
Angel Eyes

What doesn't break us makes us stronger, and once again, my saving grace was good friends for they are one of the most important things in my life.

After *Cats* and this failed relationship I returned to commercial work with pop artists and TV shows, and reconnecting with my friends, who I had lost touch with over the previous year and a half. It was that kind of relationship – the kind where you shun the friends who tell you that he may not be the right one for you. I thought they did not understand, even though they knew me best. Now I had to agree with them that they were right, while I was sobbing into my hanky, and agreeing never to do it again. Until the next time …

After that life got back on track and I decided that celibacy was the way forward – all I needed from now on would be my friends. That lasted until a night out with Jason, about a year and a half into the single life. I had not even been on a date, despite the eight-pack and the nutcracker of an ass – it was considered a crime for a gay man not to offer up his platter under those conditions but I had become content with a wank, bath and bed.

We were at Factor Twenty Five, a Sunday nightclub that started about seven and finished around one. Everyone went out early on a Sunday, which suited me fine and I would normally stay until 11, then walk home across the bridge.

We were having a great time as usual, taking the piss out of people – which was very easy to do as they got drunker throughout the night, or worse. Jason and I didn't drink, and there was no substance abuse either, and we would watch the beautiful people lose their sheen as the night wore on. I had tried alcohol once, when I was 12, and I did not like it. The humour that night came from watching people trying to behave as if they were totally sober. Within this sea of bodies I caught someone's eye as he checked me out. I did a double take, I must admit. He was not one of the messy people who kept us amused through the evening; rather he looked very serene and angelic.

Even though he was across the room, I could see that he had the most beautiful eyes. I stopped and had to look away, and I thought nothing of it. It was a momentary connection, when you feel something stronger could come of it.

I did not have much self-confidence about relationships and it never occurred to me that I could make a move on this handsome man. Call it fate, but Jason looked over and said, 'That guy keeps looking at you.' I looked over and it was heavenly eyes again, but I brushed it off and said no.

Jason, being Jason, decided he was bored with me being single (and maybe looking for a bit of time to himself to find a boyfriend). Our friendship was one that some people assumed was romantic as well, because we spent so much time together and always had a laugh.

Although I protested, Jason went over to get him. He was Spanish and his English was not very good, but with my Italian language skills we could get by. As soon as we sat down together, Jason ran off to the dance floor to join the fun.

I had a stomach roll every time I looked into the Spaniard's eyes and then I got a waft of his scent, which was amazing. I didn't realise I had moved in for the sniff and he thought I was going in for the kiss. Before I knew it, I had gone into complete meltdown, it felt so good. It felt right, as if that was how a kiss should be. I knew I wanted more than a kiss with him, and that was an unusual feeling. When we finally separated after a minute all I could see was Jason behind the Spaniard giving me the thumbs up with a big smile.

He told me that he had to go off to meet his friends, while Jason was trying to convince me that I should go home with him. I was 31, but I had never had a one-night stand. Even after that kiss and knowing I wanted more, still my insecurities kicked in after Jason's suggestion. I told myself I had no milk in the fridge for the morning – I was so desperate for an excuse to get out of it.

Come hell or high water, I was determined that it was not going to happen. I went to the bar to get Jason a cranberry and orange mix and on the way back, I saw Angel Eyes with Jason. Without a common language between them, Jason had resorted to sign language. As you can imagine, with a good dancer it was like nothing you have ever seen – there was everything except a high-kick and a spin.

When I reached them, Jason took his drink and walked off. Angel Eyes told me, in our new language, that he was

going to tell his friends that he was leaving. While he went to find his friends, I hunted down Jason and asked what he had told Angel Eyes.

Jason said: 'I told him you're going home with him tonight, and you are.' He was serious and I would have to get over my insecurities, which I forced myself to do and waited for Angel Eyes to come back.

It was an amazing experience, my first one-night stand, and with a 23-year-old! (I'm such a cougar). Ten years later, we are still together and we are married.

TWO DAYS later, I was with Jason in The Box, a formerly gay cafe and bar at Seven Dials in Covent Garden, when I got a call from Angel Eyes. At first I couldn't work out who it was because I couldn't figure out what he was saying, but I put two and two together and realised who it was.

After about five minutes, I understood that he wanted to meet up with me again. Even though I was a bit hesitant, I agreed. Already I was asking myself, is this going anywhere, do I really want this? I know the saying 'Live for the moment', but you must have had that experience when you get the second call and you think to yourself, 'Is this what I want?'

He had put so much effort into trying to ask me out for a second date that I thought it would be rude not to. I could never play it cool in my previous relationships: when I knew there was something there, I would be there an hour after the call. But not this time – I made him wait 48 hours. Actually, I felt quite empowered – it was nice to be chased. Usually I seemed to be the one doing all the chasing and trying to make things happen. It gave me confidence not having to do it this time.

When we met two days later, I didn't make any special effort. Usually I would have done the lashes, eyebrows, changed a few outfits, the new season's smellie – probably Issey Miyake. It hasn't really gone out of fashion, that lemon-fresh smell. Even though I had it, I didn't bother – not even a spray. I didn't change my clothes – and I know this is disgusting, but I didn't even brush my teeth. I just bought a pack of extra-strong mints on the way to meet him.

Even though I had had a wonderful evening on our one-night stand and he had been so sweet, I didn't have that passionate desire to see him again. I was just doing it for its own sake, because it was an evening out, rather than going home to *London Tonight*. Even though Alastair Stewart wasn't so grey then, he still wasn't a patch on Angel Eyes.

So there I was at Covent Garden, waiting opposite the tube station, all five foot seven of me. I was on full pointe, trying to see through the crowd of tall city people coming out. Suddenly I knew what my friends meant when they said they couldn't remember what their one-night stands looked like. Even though I had only been drinking cranberry, I remembered his eyes and that he shaved his head, but the rest of the features were wobbly.

Shaved heads were very popular, so every time I saw one I made an advance forward. Of course I was early – as I said, I'm never late. I decided to give him five minutes before I went home to Alastair Stewart and Mary Nightingale, too at that time.

I knew he arrived dead on six because I was watching the second hand tick around. I looked up and everything fell into place – his nose, his lips, his jaw line, and those eyes. His eyes alone were enough to make my legs wobble.

Even though I couldn't remember what he looked like, the moment I looked into his eyes as he walked towards me, I knew I was in love. Obviously it was going to take some work, but I just felt a warm feeling coming over me.

He said in broken English, 'Where we go for drink?' I wanted to say, 'My flat' – it was the first time that I had been in such a situation and I wanted to go straight home and be intimate. But I didn't say that, instead we went to a bar in Charing Cross called Qdos. We sat in the back corner and I ordered drinks. I had an orange juice this time, as the cranberry goes straight through me, and he had an alcoholic drink.

Although the conversation faltered and was slow because of the language gap, it didn't feel awkward. I felt in control because of the language barrier and all I wanted to do was kiss him. I don't normally feel comfortable doing that in public, but I leaned over and kissed him. It was so much easier than the conversation! I suppose that's why they call it the language of love.

We had been in the bar for about an hour and a half before I asked him back to my flat. I only live 10 minutes away from there and he agreed to come back with me. We had a very intimate evening, which I enjoyed more than I ever had. I was usually so self-conscious about myself, but this time I was able to forget my inhibitions and relax with him. I wasn't taking chances, though and I made sure there was some romantic music in the background, dim lighting and a few candles – you know the sort of thing. I was having a moment.

I say a moment – it went on for a few hours. The candles burned right down to the wick – and they weren't the cheap kind either, they were for guests. For some reason, the next morning when we were walking across the bridge together, I seemed to be able to understand every word he said. I think I was still floating on a cloud from the previous evening's episode. It didn't enter my head that I could be going into dangerous territory, in my usual all-or-nothing way.

Each time he opened his mouth all I could see were lots of little angels with harps and cupids, who kept piercing me with their arrows. I know I'm pushing it now, but that's how I felt at the time. He said he would call me later, after English school, and that's how I left it. I didn't even take his number – and he called me later in the day. That evening we had a repeat of the night before, and many more nights like it followed.

SIX MONTHS later I was in a relationship, by which time Angel Eyes had managed to get himself a job in a bar as his English still wasn't strong enough and in the mornings he would clean the bar.

It made me love him more, that he was such a hard worker and unpretentious in his manner.

This time round, I had made a conscious effort not to lose touch with my friends, as I had before whenever I was in a relationship. All of them seemed to love Angel Eyes as well. He was not interested in the glitz and glamour side of my life: he loved what I did, but he was not impressed by it by any means. He treated everyone the same – David, Victoria, whoever – the only thing he was interested in was me. And that's just how I liked it.

When I first introduced Mum to Angel Eyes, it was a pretty unique moment. Remember when I told you about Nanny Downer farting in her commode cupboard? This story will trump that one! When Mum first met Angel Eyes, she was taking the medication Warfarin, after she had DVT (Deep Vein Thrombosis).

Mum was in my flat when Angel Eyes arrived. She was sitting on the sofa, looking lovely and well-presented as always. Angel Eyes and I were not living together yet and Mum stood up to say hello to him. As she pushed herself off the sofa, she let one rip. It was a loud one and it seemed to go on forever. You can imagine my poor hubby did not know where to look.

I started to laugh and Mum joined in; the more she laughed, the more she farted, and the more I laughed. Angel Eyes started to laugh and it got to the point that I was having difficulty breathing and we had tears streaming down our faces. We still laugh about it today, but without the farting, thank God.

I am one of those people who like to stay at home and no matter how late I am out, I always prefer to wake up in my own bed. Angel Eyes was sharing a flat with three guys at the time and the living room was his bedroom, but I got past my usual selfishness and agreed to stay over with him, which I did, several times. It was like being a student again and I was so happy – never more so than when I was with him.

I was stressed when it came to work, as there wasn't much around. At 31, it was becoming more difficult to dance behind the younger artists and there was a new generation of dancers coming up. I was starting to consider my future in dance – and it seemed that I was reaching a crossroads in my life. Angel Eyes made it clear that it did not matter to him what I chose to do when I stopped dancing, and this gave me a great deal of confidence.

As you know, I'm not academic and I did not want to teach dance. Although I had taught, I was a selfish teacher and I did not have patience for beginners; I only wanted to work with fabulous dancers, so I wasn't cut out for that. So I decided to become a masseur – I would still be independent. I could take my business around with me; it's only a table and a bit of oil, after all. So, with the last of my savings I signed up for a massage course and I did great on the practical. As a dancer the body held no surprises for me and I was top of the class. Then came the theory and that's where I fell down, with a big bang.

I mean, there are far too many body parts! What with your ligaments, your tendons, your muscles, whatever – I'm sure those girls in Thailand on the beach haven't got any theory when they start walking all over you, and they do fine.

I might as well have burned my money – I was defeated and lost interest. I didn't even do the exams, and I beat myself up about it. But Angel Eyes was there to encourage me, working in the bar at night, cleaning in the morning, telling me he loved me, and that everything would be OK.

Another thing that always happens to me is that I could be down to my last pennies and a call would come with more work. Even though I was thinking about quitting dance, I still had people calling me for work, and thank Kylie they were!

I got a call from a friend of mine, Mark, who was with me in *Cats*. He told me about a workshop for a new show. Before a show goes into the West End, it gets workshopped on a smaller scale in a church hall somewhere then you invite producers and money people to see if they want to back it. Someone else who was in the workshop with me was Antony Cotton, from *Coronation Street*, who is very funny – I knew who he was from watching *Queer as Folk*.

The Pet Shop Boys were workshopping a new musical called *Closer to Heaven*: it really was heavenly for me, just what I needed at the time. It was about a month's work, and the pay wasn't bad. Even though I was planning to hang up my dancing shoes, I got the feeling back and I questioned my decision.

Three months later I heard that the show had found backing, which meant that it was going to be staged somewhere. But – we would have to re-audition! I had a bit of a diva strop, thinking, 'How dare they?' After all, we had created the roles – but there wasn't much work available.

During my strops Angel Eyes, whose English was much better by this time, was always very calm. He couldn't see what the problem was and his calm rubbed off on me. After all, I wasn't the one holding down two jobs and going to school.

Fortunately, I got the job after I auditioned and the show opened in the Arts Theatre in Leicester Square – a venue which was very intimate – and I loved it. The small cast was great – we were all very close. The lead lady was Frances Barber, who I grew to absolutely love. She had a great sense of humour, so quick – she could have been a gay man in a woman's body.

Even though Angel Eyes didn't want to be a part of show-business and was not impressed by the sheen, he loved theatre. He appreciated everything that went into making a show – he is the kind of audience you want. I was very excited that he was coming to see me in a show, something that he loves to do. He looked so beautiful on opening night when I met him to give him his tickets: he had dressed up for the occasion and smelled like heaven. He was more beautiful every day, and not just to me.

It felt great to be with someone who was not only pleasing on the inside, but on the outside too. I could see the gaydars on high alert when he entered a room, all six foot two of him, with his broad shoulders and tight waist, and an ass like two boiled eggs in a hanky, just waiting to be cracked. Sorry, I couldn't resist that last bit – it just seemed to flow so well.

The beginning of the show involved a lot of interaction with the audience and I was in popper-studded leather shorts and a leather harness, with leather boots up to my knees, swinging around a pole, about 10 rows into the audience, undulating over whoever was closest to my pole. And so the show went on – singing, dancing, undulating.

The show was about many things, one of them being a straight boy who has an affair with a gay guy and then becomes very confused. It happens in the real world too, believe it or not. There were prostitutes and junkies in the show – the usual characters you find in that genre. I guess that's why it was called *Closer to Heaven* – they were living on the edge.

The first night was a huge success, the audience were on their feet, clapping and stamping. I think some audience members might have done other things as well – I'm just

glad I wasn't working front of house, having to clean up that mess.

After the show I met Angel Eyes and he was so proud and emotional that he had tears in his eyes. That's something I love about Latino men – they aren't frightened of their emotions. After he told me how proud he was, and how much he enjoyed the show, he made it very clear that he wasn't happy with me undulating in the audience. It made me feel quite fluttery that this big hunk of a gorgeous man, who everyone looked at, was jealous of me. It was a wonderful feeling, more so because he was not concerned with his own beauty – he saw only the audience looking at me.

It was a shame that the show did not have a very long run – I guess the subject matter was not to everyone's taste, but Angel Eyes absolutely loved it and was very supportive. He came to see the show 27 times. I like to think it wasn't just because of his love for the show: perhaps his need to keep an eye on the audience and make sure no-one got too close had something to do with it.

There I was after the show had closed, once again asking myself what to do. Should I continue in showbusiness or leave and get a normal job? I don't think I need to explain what I mean by normal, do I?

19

Pineapple

I had been going to Pineapple for years – to do class, audition and rehearse – and I knew all the staff. I was quite friendly with the manager and I would often sit in her office after rehearsal or class and we would put the world to rights. One day after class when we were chatting, I told her I was not sure about my future; I was so content and happy with Angel Eyes, I didn't feel that I would miss out on anything. Life was rich, and I was with someone who loved me and cared about me, and I thought this was the perfect time to make the change from being a professional dancer to doing … I had no idea what.

I knew that I had to finish on a high because I did not want to audition for jobs that I was too old for. It's the reality of the business – there was a new generation of dancers coming up. I was one of those dancers who had managed to live his dream – I had been in West End shows and toured with the biggest pop acts in the world.

My contemporaries knew me as a great dancer and that is how I wanted to be remembered, not as some old hoofer who was still trying to hang on as a performer. I thought a PAYE job would be perfect – I wouldn't have to worry about sorting out my own tax and all the other things you have to take care of yourself when you are a performer.

That's when the manager at Pineapple asked me if I would like a job at the studios, working on the reception desk. I said 'yes' straightaway, and it wasn't until I left that I asked myself if I had made the right decision. I had been at the top of my profession and I knew everyone in the building – what would they think when they came in and saw me in reception? It seemed like a step down.

Angel Eyes pointed out that I would be happy: it was a job, it would mean not having to worry about the day-to-day things. He made it sound so perfect – what did it matter what I did, as long as I was happy? And I *was* happy.

Saying that, on my first day almost everyone who walked through the door looked at me in amazement. Many people thought I was joking, while some laughed nervously, and others came right out and asked me what the hell I was doing behind reception.

The funny thing was that I didn't care. I couldn't have done it five years earlier, after touring with the Spice Girls and performing in *Cats*, because I also looked down on the work – it did not enter my head that I would ever have to do anything like that.

THE FIRST week at Pineapple was difficult, although I did not care about the people who did look down on me for doing a job that I was enjoying and that gave me security. It was the administrative duties that got to me – you had to count beyond five, six, seven, eight! There was banking to be done, cashing up, etc. But I turned it into a choreography – things just had to be done in a certain way. I started to enjoy it, and felt I was learning and enjoying it in a way that I had not experienced when I was younger.

Coming from a dance background, I wanted to do everything well and I treated it as a performance. Some of the staff did not have that enthusiasm for the role, nor the discipline that came from a performance background. This was noticed eventually, and although we were all receptionists, some of them started to follow my lead.

It helped that I knew everyone coming into the building, but I was just old enough to remember the previous generation of choreographers and dancers, so I was able to make everyone welcome. Those who were not so en vogue were made to feel as welcome as the latest hot choreographer. I started to give advice on which new teachers should be hired, and the styles of dance that ought to be included in the timetable. I began to look for dancers and choreographers for any events that Pineapple would put on and generally made sure that the shows were of a standard that would be expected of such a well-known studio.

One event I staged was a fashion show at The Hurlingham Club and it was hosted by Pineapple's founder, Debbie Moore, OBE. We spent a lot of time together preparing for the show, sorting out the music, dancers, clothing, etc. The show was perfect and Debbie called me into her office the next day and said she would like to promote me, and gave me my new title, artistic director. This did not really change the nature of my work, but she recognised that I took initiative and that I knew everyone who came through the doors. This could only be good for business.

I HAD been artistic director for about six months when I received an email from a production company. They were looking for judges for a new dance show they were starting on Trouble TV. They wanted someone with a big CV, choreography skills and a big personality. I thought they must mean me! It came with an advert that they asked me to place on the audition board and I'm not ashamed to say that I did not put it on the board. As soon as I saw the advert, I had the urge to perform again.

The judging role seemed the perfect outlet, so I sent along my information, feeling very confident that I would get a call quick sticks. Well, did I? No, I didn't! There was nothing quick about it, and while I was waiting to hear back, others were telling me they were up for the same job.

You can't keep anything quiet in the industry, and I should have known that it would not just have come to me at Pineapple. A showbiz secret is one that everyone knows and I found out that they had selected two choreographer/judges for the show who could battle against each other.

The show was going to be called *Bump'n'Grind* – I'm sure some of you remember it. I must admit that I was a bit disappointed, but I was not devastated. I had a good job that I enjoyed, and Angel Eyes and I were still very much in love.

So, I thought nothing else of it and hoped the show was a complete failure. I wouldn't have been able to watch myself anyway, as I did not have Sky or cable TV.

I got a call from the production company after the show had started airing. They wanted an expert to give an opinion on aspects of the show – which I was tempted to turn down. I thought, what's wrong with the experts you have? Did you not choose the right people? I said politely that I would love to take part in the show. Two years after my last performance and I was thrown back into the great wardrobe dilemma. At this point I was in my tight-cut-off-tee phase and my arms were looking particularly good.

Once I got my wardrobe together, I was set and ready to go. It was lights, camera, action!

20
Bump'n'Grind

It felt so right and I did not feel nervous for a moment – I felt as if I should be there. The show was about dance, and I *was* dance.

I don't know what I did, or what I said, but it must have been good. As soon as I left the studio, I had all the producers around me. They told me what a great job I had done and asked if I would like to come back on the show. But I didn't point out that they had turned me down first time around – I had made my point. I was right when I saw the email – I was right for that job, and now they knew it too.

I returned many times on the show as an expert, and when it came to the second season, I had successfully taken over. Along with another choreographer, I was now mentoring and leading a group of dancers; we battled it out for the competition prize. 'Why start a fight if you know you are not going to win?' quickly became my motto. Let's just say I was never frightened to start a fight, and I always won.

I think the key to my success was not being selfish and not thinking I could do it all myself. This was what the other choreographer did; but I just wanted to win, so I got the best group of choreographers I could to work with my dancers, to show their versatility – this always won the fight.

The show ran for three years and I'm pleased to say that I won every year. This was my first insight into the world of TV. It was very different to my experience on TV as a musical theatre performer or dancer. There seemed to be no loyalty or emotion involved; the producers and everyone involved in a show will do anything and say anything to get the best show they can, and as soon as it's finished, they move on to the next project and it starts all over again.

I found that a little bit difficult to deal with as I work with my emotions. The term I use to describe these people is TV Wankers.

For one of the finals I wanted my group of dancers to be dressed alike, which would have made the performance and choreography look stronger. They told me they did not have a budget for it and I found it difficult to understand that they could not spend 20 or 30 pounds on some tee-shirts for the dancers. No-one fought my corner, and I bought the clothing out of my own money; I had become emotionally involved, but they didn't care – it was just a job to them.

I tried to adapt to that way of working, but I realised I did not want to change if it meant that I would turn into a TV Wanker. I am quite sure that some of them thought the same about me, and that I was just being difficult, but I can't let something go if I think it is going to be damaging to the overall picture.

ONE OF the great things about working at Pineapple was that they were very understanding if a job like this came in – they would give me time off to do it. I would also make sure that all of the rehearsals were at Pineapple, so it was good for business. I did this show for three years, and I felt I had quite a bit of experience and understanding of this genre. I had mentored and choreographed dancers for all those years.

So, when a primetime TV show came along, called *Strictly Dance Fever*, I thought I was in with a good chance. I sent my information off to them, but I heard absolutely nothing. Fortunately for me, working at Pineapple I would get to see and hear everything; it would only be a matter of time until they had to come in. When they eventually came in, I was very nice and accommodating, as I was with all clients.

I slipped it in very subtly that I had sent in my CV and asked if they had received it. They asked my name and when I told them, they said yes, but they had so many to go through. I knew they didn't have a clue who I was, and were just being polite – they probably hadn't printed it off.

They were seeing people throughout the day and I could see some who I knew weren't right for the job. They could not have choreographed their way out of *Flashdance*; but they kept coming.

As they were packing up to leave, I slipped into the studio to tidy up and casually asked as I was tidying around them, if they had had a successful day. I find that manner seems to work – it opens people up, and makes it seem as if you care, when you really don't. As usual, it worked and they started talking. They said it had not been a bad day – there were one or two, but they still needed to look for other people. Before

I could remind them that they had still not looked at my CV, the one with the bad perm asked me if I knew of anyone else. Did I know any people that could be sent to see them?

Being artistic director, which was the hat I was wearing at that time, I had to remain calm and composed. My first reaction was, 'Yes, *Me*! I can do it standing on my head, doing the splits!' But I decided it was probably best not to do it, and despite my horror and rage, I asked for her email address. It's always a good move, to get close to the source.

I gathered a few names together, not forgetting to include mine, and I should have known – TV Wankers again. Not even a thank you and not even a look-in.

SOMEONE I recommended was chosen for the show and I decided I did not have the right to be bitter. I had a good job that I enjoyed, but these TV adventures gave me a great deal of pleasure and fulfilled my desire to still perform. But in truth, every day at Pineapple was a performance – you just can't help yourself when you are surrounded by so much glitz and glamour. That's what I loved about working there – it was full of wonderful people. There was always something exciting happening, and always new people coming in. And there was never a dull moment – certainly not while I was around.

We would often break out into a full-on dance routine at reception, with me in lead, of course. Because it was always full of performers, it was never difficult to find people to join in, or we just basked in their glow as they glided by to their studios, whether it was VB changing in the office and slipping out the back door to avoid the paparazzi or the heavenly Kylie leaving a trail of broken hearts as she left us with a big smile.

Talking of broken hearts – not that my heart was ever broken by any of those TV jobs that I didn't get – I received yet another email in my inbox. Sky1 were looking for judges for a new primetime show, someone with dance and circus skills.

21
Cirque de Celebrité

I didn't have any circus skills, other than clowning around now and then, but these days they seem to put anything in a circus. It's no longer just lion taming or riding a horse around the ring with a teacup balanced on your head.

But I was North Essex trampoline champion aged 12, and I had acrobatic skills – there are acrobats in the circus. And I can walk downstairs on my hands, with my feet over my head, while talking out of my ass. Now, that's unique. Once again, I did not post the notice on the audition board. I updated my CV, adjusting my circus skills by adding a few at random, sent it on its way through cyberspace and waited for a reply, with no great expectation.

It always seems to be the way, doesn't it? When you have no expectations, things start to happen. As soon as my CV went out into cyberspace, I got a reply. This could have been for one of two reasons: they are seeing everyone who applies, or the show is so crap that no-one had bothered to reply.

Either way, I was happy to get a reply. If I got the job, I could put it down to experience and I like a challenge. I was 12 the last time I went to the circus, but I found it quite pleasant watching all those acrobats walking around in their tight pants without any visible means of support. It gave a whole new meaning to 'meat and two veg' when I saw them suspended in the air – it was the only time I found gravity appealing.

I had a time and a date to see some TV execs about the new circus show. I found it a bit inconvenient having to go out into the sticks to the Sky offices, as the show was to be aired on Sky1. Now, I'm not one for travel – my 10-minute walk into work is usually enough for me – and I nearly had second thoughts about going. But of course I went, on the great British Transport – it took me about five hours to get to the edge of the city and just beyond.

When I arrived, I had to take the lift to the fifth floor. I'm not a lift person either, but I didn't want to seem demanding at the beginning, so I gritted my teeth and bore it. It's not the way to begin an interview, hyperventilating and out of breath, and I thought I'd get five minutes to catch my breath and have a glass of water. I needed a little time to regulate my breath, but instead they shuffled me straight into the offices of Richard Woolfe. He was very important at Sky, but I didn't have a clue.

He was very bubbly and jolly, and not at all stuffy and corporate. He explained the format of the show, which was to be called *Cirque de Celebrité* – celebrities performing circus acts, to be voted on by the public, with input from the judges. It all seemed to be going very well – they were impressed with my dance CV.

I didn't give them time to get a word in after that; I told them that circus had changed, with Cirque du Soleil as the prime example, and with my knowledge of acrobatics, I would have some empathy for the contestants.

Of course, in his office the size of a postage stamp, I had to do a few pirouettes, a backflip and wrapped my leg around my neck, pulling my leg around my head. I was pretty confident this may have sealed the deal but then again, you can never tell with the TVWs.

I thought I'd bagged it but on the train home, I started going back through everything I had done in the interview. By the time I got back, not only was I not going to get the job, I never even wanted it in the first place. This was a useful outcome, as it meant that I wouldn't spend every minute checking my emails.

Just as well I did, because I had forgotten about the job when I got a call a month later. Apparently I was on the shortlist and they wanted me to meet the production company. It can be such a pain dealing with this in-between bit – much better either not to get the job, or to get it outright. Luckily for me, the production company was in Covent Garden, so it was easy.

Then the games began. Because the production companies get their money from the broadcaster, they will try and get you for nothing. From my brief experience on *Bump'n'Grind*, I knew they would start by offering me nothing, then I would say I wasn't interested. They would come back with crap, I would say no, and they would come back with a bit more on top of the crap. This is exactly what happened, and I settled on the crap money, which was at least better than the crap, crap money.

I would only be needed on Sunday evenings, and I didn't do much on Sundays – only going to the gym and watching three hours of Catherine Cookson on the telly while the Marks roast was cooking in the oven. I figured I wouldn't be missing out on much by sitting in a big top, in a wet and muddy field, surrounded by multi-national acrobats swinging on a trapeze.

I really enjoyed the show and I thought the contestants dealt well with what were actually quite challenging tasks. Mainly I judged them on their acrobatic skills and the choreographic content. We were three judges in total – one of them owned the circus and the other was a circus performer, so they could deal with the circus side of the evening.

AS QUICKLY as the show started, it seemed to finish. I was ready for it to come to an end; the show aired right up to Christmas, so I was happy to leave the icy winds and snow-storms behind, and the big top heated by a generator that kept breaking down.

The show was a success, but I don't think it was a great success – the viewing figures weren't amazing. There was talk at the end of the run that the producers were thinking of bringing it back for a second series the following year. Richard Woolfe, who had commissioned it, told me that he thought I did a great job and he definitely wanted me back. He thought I brought a spark and humour to the show. I told him I would love to do another series, but they would have to do something about the money.

My theory is they can have you the first time for a pittance, but once you've proved your worth, they need to start flashing the cash. That's what they did not do when they contacted me a year later. They told me they wanted me on the show again, and that I brought something extra to it but they weren't going to offer me any more money. I didn't want to be a sycophant – that's quite a big word for me. It means an ass-licker (I only learned it a couple of years ago).

Now, I'm not greedy, but I know my worth and the extra cash came in handy in the season of goodwill to all men. The extra jobs that I did outside Pineapple went into my savings, for home repairs and for holidays with Angel Eyes – it was my safety net.

The production company did not see it that way – they thought they were doing me a favour by letting me appear on TV. As you can imagine, we did not come to an agreement – I turned the job down. I was not about to sell myself down the swanee, forget that.

I then got a call from Richard Woolfe at Sky, who wanted to know why I wasn't doing the job. Now that's the kind of person you want to deal with in a negotiation – someone who says, 'Leave it with me – what do you want?' I would have understood if I was being greedy, but I wasn't. Richard fought my corner and made it very clear that he wanted me on the show for the money I was asking, and that's how I came to agree to take part in the second series.

SERIES 2 of *Cirque de Celebrité* was a great show, but it just didn't get the viewing figures and if they don't get the viewing figures, they scrap it. As I said, it was just extra for me, so I wasn't too worried: I had my job at Pineapple – I was not unemployed.

I met some lovely people working on the show – it wasn't all about the acrobats. Ruby Wax was the ringmaster on the first series and our dressing rooms were next to each other. I say dressing room – it wasn't a Winnebago. It was more like a portaloo without the toilet, very cold and uninviting. That's why I used to like to hang out with Rubes, chatting about this, that and everything. She has studied psychology and I was always worried I was being analysed, but I don't think her training had prepared her for someone like me – I'm not prepared for myself sometimes.

Ruby didn't present the second series, I'm not sure why. The second series was presented by Jenni Falconer from GMTV. She used to present the entertainment section on that show with Ben Shephard.

Jenni was lovely, very down-to-earth, and I really enjoyed working with her. It's better to work with people like that – some people are so into themselves, they don't have time to see you. It also makes a show run more smoothly – everyone is then willing to give everything they can. I think it's damaging when you have people who think they are more important than they really are. If I were employing people like that, I don't care how famous they were – they wouldn't get the job.

It's amazing what you get to see sometimes, when you are on the inside. You get to see how pathetic and deluded some celebrities can be. We did not have A-list celebrities on the show – as you can imagine, swinging from a trapeze by your ponytail isn't going to appeal to someone like Cheryl Cole.

Sinitta was a lovely guest on the show, and Kenzie too. There were one or two who thought they should have been at the beginning and not the end of the celebrity alphabet but their attitude and behaviour to others pushed them right off the alphabet for me – they were rude to everyone on the show and did not contribute to any of the group performances. My job was much more pleasurable when those people weren't around – this was where I enjoyed my role as judge, helping the public to vote off those contestants.

Unlike the first season, at the end of Season 2 they made it very clear that there would not be a third series of *Cirque de Celebrité*. Once again, it was not a problem for me – I just went back to my day job.

22

The Seven-Year Hitch

Life at Pineapple was great, as usual, and I loved my job more and more every day. I never thought that after I stopped dancing, I would enjoy doing anything as much as I enjoyed working at Pineapple. I don't feel that I have ever worked a day in my life because I have loved everything I have done.

Being at Pineapple meant that I was constantly surrounded by what I loved. Even though I had chosen to give up dance, I was still in touch at Pineapple with what was current. I knew about the latest choreographers, dancers and dance styles. There still isn't anything going on in the dance world that I don't know about. Even though I had stopped dancing professionally, I could never quit. I often did classes at Pineapple because it kept me in very good shape and it is still when I feel most alive, being at one with the music. It was also reassuring to know that I could still do it. I would deliberately stand beside the dancers new out of college, who were used to eight-hour days, just to prove to myself that I still had it. Experience counts for a lot, but I also wanted to know that I could still get my legs higher – I don't think I will ever get rid of that competitive streak.

Even now, when I do a class, I tell myself it doesn't matter if I can't turn as fast or jump so high – as soon as the class starts, it is a battle and the fight begins. Even though I'm more than twice the age of some of the dancers, I can still win. It's good for the young ones anyway, having someone to measure themselves against – not in height, obviously. That's one battle I never win. It was what made me hungry as a young dancer, focussing on the other dancers I wanted to dance like. I feel I'm providing a service sometimes by being the oldest dancer in the class: it gives me a great feeling of worth to think that some of these young dancers may be looking up to me, the way I looked up to older dancers when I was their age.

I find it funny now when these young dancers come up to me now and say, 'I can't believe you can still dance like that for your age,' because I look at them and I don't feel any different to them. I guess everyone of a certain age has experienced that – on the inside you still feel like 20, it's just the exterior that gives it away.

It is in those moments that I find it hard to believe that 20 years have gone that really seem like yesterday. I look at these young kids and I want to suck the lifeblood out of them – of course I don't mean that. I just make sure I go across the floor with them next time and let them know who is boss – I may be old, but I can still knock it out like the best of 'em.

What I find amusing is the shock on their faces when they see me in class, and I can dance. They only know me from the reception and taking their entry fees. It reminds me of Carmine and me in our younger days; there were no dancers before us, and there would not be any following after us – no-one else existed. But there were people after us, and there will be after these youngsters. In my mind everyone knows I was a dancer – I guess it's an age thing, assuming the word would still be going around, 10 years after I have given up. But no, I have to get my Lycra and crop tops out to keep my name alive. 'It's a hard knock life,' to quote young Annie.

ON TOP of having to keep my name alive in the dance world, on the seventh anniversary of Angel Eyes and I meeting, he only went and asked me to marry him. They say seven years can make or break a relationship, when you start to get itchy. There was nothing itchy about us, apart from my eczema, which would kick in now and then if I went too heavily on the mature Cheddar. I do love a good toasted cheese and pickle.

No itching for us – we were still blissfully in love. Angel Eyes had moved in a year after we met, so we had been living together for six years. I know some of you are thinking I must be joking, but I'm not. After all that time of living together in a small flat, our relationship still felt very fresh to me. We still said we loved each other every day and yes, it was partly habitual, but we still meant it.

He was very much a part of the Spence family by then and got on very well with them all. My sisters made it very clear that they thought he was hot and if he ever wanted to turn, I could leave him with them. I think if we had split up, then they would have kept him and let me loose to fend for myself.

Louie Spence

I was so surprised when he asked me to marry him – I say 'marry' and I know it's a civil partnership, but to us it's a marriage. On our anniversary he wrote a poem on a scroll, tied with a red ribbon. I opened it and read up to the point where he asked me to marry him.

> *To Louie*
> *Seven years I have been next to you,*
> *Seven years of merging, happiness and comfort,*
> *Seven years of lows, ups and uppers.*
> *Seven years of understanding, support and forgiveness*
> *Seven years of love*
> *Seven years of you.*
> *Another seven I want, another seven I ask for.*
> *Can I have them? Don't answer yet.*
> *Of questions, the world is full,*
> *Some can be answered, some cannot*
> *Sometimes it's cool to say I know not.*
> *On one, now, I wish to display,*
> *Without any fear of being called gay.*
> *Since these last seven years,*
> *Have been wonderful with thee,*
> *I wanted to ask you,*
> *Would you like to marry me?*

I did not know what to say. I re-read it to myself, because I sometimes jump ahead when I read and things don't make sense.

The second time around and I knew I had read it correctly. He was standing in front of me with a big smile on his face. I thought to myself, 'Well, I can't say no, now.' Not that I would have said no, but that's the thought that went through my head. It must have shown on my face and he thought I was hesitating because I had not said yes straightaway; it was only because I had to read it twice to make sure. So we had to have a small argument about this beautiful moment and it went a little bit pear-shaped due to my slow response.

After a couple of hours of sulking, we settled on a date for the event. I was very excited until I started to think about the preparations. I am like a goldfish – I have no patience, and I like things to be instant. Angel Eyes loved the budgeting and the planning, and if I couldn't get excited about the event it might look as if I wasn't interested. What a life!

Previously, my view of marriage was that it was just a piece of paper – if you loved each other, you just needed to stay together. And my experience of gay relationships was that people only stayed together if they wanted to be with each other – there were fewer of the reasons, such as kids or a mortgage, that straight people often expressed for staying together. It was not until I was put in the situation that I developed another view and marriage began to mean more to me.

The arrangements alone made us closer. If not, they certainly would have driven us apart – I'm surprised any weddings take place at all. I found it very stressful, as we were arranging everything ourselves. Whatever he wanted, I wanted nothing to do with, and vice versa. I thought we would just have to pay and then get married, but first we had to register with the local authority. Then we had an interview at the town hall and they asked us questions like, how long had we been together. I know Angel Eyes is Spanish, but Spain is part of the EU, so I didn't understand the point of that. We were interviewed separately and had to answer questions about each other's names, pastimes, nicknames and other personal information. It annoyed me that we had to go through this process. We had provided proof that we had been living together for six years and I thought it was a waste of time.

Anyway, it had to be done and once we had been approved, we were allowed to book a registrar. Before we could book a registrar, we had to know the date we would like to get married but we had not decided on a venue. I did not want to get married at a registry office then move on somewhere else; I wanted it all in one place, otherwise I knew I would spend the whole day worrying about everyone. Angel Eyes' family would be arriving from Spain for the wedding and they don't all speak English, so I wanted it to be easy for them as well. With my attention span, you can imagine how bored I was by all this planning. We eventually found a venue in the West End, which was a restaurant that used to be old courtrooms, so they had a licence to host weddings and they also had function rooms. That was one of the major things out of the way.

The next thing was finding accommodation for everyone that would be near the venue and affordable. This was going to be difficult as they all needed to be close to the venue. We would need about 20 rooms, so I contacted lots of hotels, assuming I would be able to get a discount. Our wedding fell on the Bank Holiday weekend in August, so it was hard enough to get a room, let alone a discount.

Our families were not fussy, their main demand was somewhere clean and close to the venue. I had noticed a pub around the corner from me that also had reasonable accommodation, so I went to check it out with Angel Eyes and it was perfect. They had 21 rooms, so we booked the lot. They gave us a nice little discount into the bargain.

So, venue – check, accommodation – check, registrar – check. The last major decision was my dress. Now, it did cross my mind but I thought I didn't want to shock the Spanish family, even though I still had the waistline to carry off white. Angel Eyes had made up his mind to wear a dinner suit with cummerbund, bow tie, the works. But I don't like wearing dinner suits and I didn't want us to look like His'n'His: I wanted to bring a bit of colour into the occasion. I spent weeks traipsing around the shops trying on endless outfits before I finally decided on a very fine midnight-blue corduroy suit, which looked more like velvet. I teamed it with a pink shirt and a big ruffled bow – very New Romantic or Edwardian, however you want to look at it. It was not a white dress, but I looked very elegant.

I couldn't believe how stressed I was getting as the day drew closer, following up on RSVPs so that we could let the caterers know how many people to expect. We definitely could not afford a free bar all evening, so we had to work out how much alcohol we were going to pay for. My family alone could drink the vineyards of France dry.

AFTER ALL the stress and planning, the day arrived. Everyone was settled into their accommodation, and both our families had arrived the night before, so all they had to do was get in cabs and make their way to the venue, which took five minutes. I went early to the venue with Angel Eyes;

there was a little room where we could change into our attire and I had a giggle to myself. When I looked around at all the flower arrangements, I thought to myself getting married was the one thing I never thought I would do.

Weddings have never been my favourite events – something is always bound to go wrong when you put people together who have made a point of avoiding each other for a few years and then get them drunk. I don't know about your family, but mine could be trouble. I definitely did not want a sit-down meal with speeches and people trying to be funny when they weren't. Also, I didn't want a long ceremony – I wanted it to be fun … I keep on saying 'I' don't I? Angel Eyes did have a say in it and I/we wanted the ceremony to be relaxed. It did not bother me that we could not have any religious songs at our civil ceremony as I only know 'Away in a Manger'.

As people arrived we had a mixture of Whitney, Babs, and a collection of show tunes. Guests were greeted at the door by the Ice Queen, as I affectionately call him, Mr Jason Gardiner – and Carmine, of course. There were no flowers in lapels – there was just one bloom that day, and it was me. The good thing about having Carmine on the door was that he could parcel everyone up in several languages and if they did not understand him, Jason would just shout at them. Pat, my mum, was to give me away on the day and she was your typical Mother of the Bride. She complained about her outfit while downing a quadruple Bacardi with a dash of Coke – for Dutch courage, you understand. Angel Eyes was to walk down the aisle with his sister Belen.

While Pat attacked her second Bacardi, I started to slip into my outfit. The registrar arrived as I was about to step into my trousers: she wanted to run through the ceremony with me, while I was standing in my pink shirt, ruffles, and socks and pants. I did not think it was appropriate to go through the vows only half-dressed, so I tied my belt around my waist and over my shirt, and then we went through the nuptials. Luckily for me, she was a lovely lady with a great sense of humour: she was going to need it.

After we had discussed everything, she told us we had five minutes. It was like being back in the theatre again: 'Ladies and gentlemen, this is your five-minute call, five minutes, you have five minutes.'

At this point I started to feel a little bit nervous. That was when I realised it was not a performance, it was real. Even though I knew my family were very open about my sexuality and they all loved Angel Eyes, it felt strange for me. I wondered how they would look at us – two men getting married. Would Dad sit there and wish for a straight son? Angel Eye's father did not come to the wedding; he gave him his blessing, but he does not like to fly, and I totally understand that.

We were waiting outside the doors, ready to walk down the aisle to our choice of music. But before that, we had an overture, 'I'm Not Getting Married Today' from *Company* by Stephen Sondheim. All the theatricals in the audience laughed at this. My family did not have a clue and Angel Eyes' family did not understand a word, but it made us laugh and helped kill some of our nerves.

Once the overture finished, the doors opened and we began our slow march down the aisle – me and Mum, and Angel Eyes with his sister. The aisle was not wide enough to fit us all, so he went first and I entered second, of course. I made my way to his side and the ceremony began.

Louie Spence

We started the proceedings in a very formal manner and everyone remained seated while we each played a song we had chosen for each other. I played 'Lovin' You' by Minnie Riperton, which got them all going – especially the girls from Essex. Angel Eyes chose 'Your Song' by Elton John, which finished them off. Who needs 'Morning Has Broken' or 'Kumbaya', when you have Minnie and Elton?

Lovin' You
(by Minnie Riperton and Richard Rudolph)

Lovin' you
Is easy 'cause you're beautiful …
Making love with you
Is all I want to do …
Lovin' you
Is more than just a dream come true …
And everything that I do
Is out of lovin' you …

No-one else can make me feel
The colours that you bring …
Stay with me while we grow old …
And we will live each day in spring time …

STILL GOT IT, NEVER LOST IT!

Because lovin' you ...
Has made my life so beautiful ...
And every day of my life
Is filled with loving you ...
Lovin' you ...
I see your soul come shining through ...
And everytime that we ...
Oh, I'm more in love with you ...

Your Song
(by Elton John and Bernie Taupin)

It's a little bit funny, this feeling inside
I'm not one of those who can easily hide
I don't have much money, but boy if I did
I'd buy a big house where we both could live

If I was a sculptor, but then again, no
Or a man who makes potions in a travelling show
I know it's not much but it's the best I can do
My gift is my song and this one's for you

And you can tell everybody this is your song
It may be quite simple but now that it's done
I hope you don't mind
I hope you don't mind that I put down in words
How wonderful life is while you're in the world

I sat on the roof and kicked off the moss
Well, a few of the verses well, they've got me quite cross
But the sun's been quite kind while I wrote this song
It's for people like you that keep it turned on

So excuse me forgetting but these things I do
You see I've forgotten if they're green or they're blue
Anyway the thing is what I really mean
Yours are the sweetest eyes I've ever seen

After everyone had composed themselves there were some more formalities before I read a little poem. Don't ask me where it came from, but after the first two lines I came over all emotional. It really came from nowhere and it shocked me – I had to do a half turn with my back to the room while I got myself together for a second or two. It did not stop however, so I just let it flow. It was an emotional poem filled with love.

I was sort of hoping,
That you would come along,
Like the answer to a prayer,
And the music to a song.

Like the kind of thing that happens,
At a special place and time,
That will change our lives forever,
Like a fantasy of mine.

The fantasy was there before,
I ever knew your name,
And now that I have found you,
We will never be the same.

So, pardon, if I look at you,
Forgive me if I stare,
At the fantasy I knew before,
I saw you standing there.

For I was always hoping,
That you would come along,
Like the answer to a prayer,
And the music to a song.

Angel Eyes got his best friend to read a poem of his choosing in Spanish (we had to cater for everyone). By this point, even though my family did not understand a word, they were emotionally overwhelmed and there was a bit of wailing in the room.

Si el hombre pudiera decir lo que ama
(by Luis Cernuda)

Si el hombre pudiera decir lo que ama,
si el hombre pudiera levantar su amor por el cielo
como una nube en la luz;
si como muros que se derrumban,
para saludar la verdad erguida en medio,
pudiera derrumbar su cuerpo,
dejando sólo la verdad de su amor,

la verdad de sí mismo,
que no se llama gloria, fortuna o ambición,
sino amor o deseo,
yo sería aquel que imaginaba;
aquel que con su lengua, sus ojos y sus manos
proclama ante los hombres la verdad ignorada,
la verdad de su amor verdadero.

Libertad no conozco sino la libertad de estar preso en
    alguien
cuyo nombre no puedo oír sin escalofrío;
alguien por quien me olvido de esta existencia mezquina
por quien el día y la noche son para mí lo que quiera,
y mi cuerpo y espíritu flotan en su cuerpo y espíritu
como leños perdidos que el mar anega o levanta
libremente, con la libertad del amor,
a única libertad que me exalta,
la única libertad por que muero.

Tú justificas mi existencia:
si no te conozco, no he vivido;
si muero sin conocerte, no muero, porque no he vivido.

If a Man Could Say How Much He Loves
(by Luis Cernuda – English translation)

If a man could say how much he loves,
If a man could raise his love in the sky
like a cloud in the light;
if like falling walls,
in order to salute the truth, straightened in the middle,

he could plunge his body headlong,
leaving just the truth about his love,
the truth about himself,
which is not called glory, nor fortune, nor ambition,
but love or desire,
I would be the one who imagined;
the one who, with his tongue, his eyes and his hands,
proclaims in front of the men the ignored truth,
the truth about his true love.

Freedom I do not know but the freedom of being
    imprisoned in anybody
whose name I cannot hear without chill;
someone for whom I forget this mean existence,
for whom the day and the night are for me whatever he
    wants,
and my body and spirit float in his body and spirit
like lost logs that the sea submerges or raises
freely, with the freedom of love,
the only freedom that exalts me,
the only truth for which I die.

You justify my existence:
if I do not meet you, I haven't lived;
if I die without meeting you, I don't die, because I haven't
    lived.

Before we knew it, we were exchanging rings. We had a
quick kiss before signing the register. My witness was not
Carmine, even though he was my oldest friend, and it was
not Jason: it was the first love of my life, Piero.

I could not think of anyone better than Piero, who knew me so well – not just as a friend, but intimately. Even though we had experienced ups and downs, and had a period of non-communication after we separated, we had grown up and experienced many things together. We had become like brothers over the years and our relationship was unbreakable: there was nothing he would not do for me and I would do anything for him.

As we got older, we realised we were much better suited as friends than as lovers. We share a wonderful relationship, and both care about our partners, and my life is richer because I can still share it with him.

ONCE WE had signed the register, I stood and held court. And as the venue was an old courtroom, I was judge and jury. Everyone was relaxed and thoroughly enjoyed the ceremony, and the food was great – we had decided on a buffet. I was waiting, and it did happen: my Auntie Shirley came up to me and said, 'Ooh, it's a lovely spread.'

Angel Eyes looked so proud and happy, and it meant so much to him to have all his family there. Whereas it had been quite clear to my family from day one that I was gay, I don't think it was the same for Angel Eyes and his family. He only told them he was gay after he asked me to marry him (I think I was more frightened of their reaction than he was). His family is very close and loving, they are very kind and caring people: I really was not sure how his dad was going to react, as he is very old school.

Even though I had been back and forth to Spain with Angel Eyes several times over the last five years, I was still not sure that his dad had clicked. I suppose that was me being stupid – how could you think that someone who is in their seventies had not come across gay people before? I was still surprised that his dad knew what was coming next, when Angel Eyes told him he was getting married.

Although I'm sure it was very difficult for him, he was very kind and gracious, and he gave us his blessing. I think it was obvious to him that we loved each other, and how happy and content Angel Eyes was in our relationship. His dad may not have been at the wedding, but the rest of his family had a ball. They all danced alongside my family and I was worried when the reggae came on that Mum might break into a bit of dancehall, but she didn't, thank goodness. In fact, I noticed that she had gone missing at some point in the night, along with my sisters. Being me, I panicked and thought the worst – nothing specific, but I just thought something had to happen on this wonderful day.

After searching the two floors, I found them outside sitting on the pavement with their shoes off, having a fag – so council, but I love it. I'm glad to say she's stopped that now – the smoking that is (the shoes still come off at weddings).

I had my two-glass quota of rosé at the ceremony, while everyone else indulged. This was not just a wedding; it was their first gay wedding. Not only that, it was in the West End of London. They were not going to waste an opportunity to make the most of their night out.

All I can say is that it was an absolute hit and everyone had an amazing time, except me. Don't get me wrong, I was happy on the inside but being me, once the ceremony was over, I went into my usual mode. I was worried about what my nephews were getting up to, what the caterers were getting up to, and pretty much anything I could find to worry about.

I was most worried about Angel Eyes' family, particularly that they would all get back to their accommodation okay. I had planned to hire a minibus, but he said taxis would be fine. Of course, when the time came to leave, there was not a cab in sight. His family had no clue where they were going, and even if my family had a clue where they themselves were heading, their legs were not taking them in the right direction. They had all had one too many, and left was right and right was left.

So, everyone had to march back on foot, 20 minutes over the bridge, which took about an hour and a half. I felt like a sheepdog, trying to round up the stragglers, and those who kept drifting off. After I got the ring on my finger, I had turned into a neurotic bride. Angel Eyes was relaxed and enjoying himself with his family, while I spun round in ever-decreasing circles.

Everyone got back to their pub accommodation in one piece and I could finally breathe. All I wanted to do was go home and go to bed, not before having an argument with Angel Eyes. Looking back now, I was a total nag and I think I would have slapped myself, had I been him. I had a go at him for leaving everything to me and not looking after his family by making sure they got back safely. Of course I was being a control freak as they were all well-travelled adults, who could easily have made their own way back.

THE NEXT morning we met up for breakfast with his family and I arranged a minibus to get them to the airport – no relying on taxis this time. Once I had packed his family off, I was left with mine and they were easy to deal with – they could just hop in their cars and head back home, to my relief. It's not that I don't love them: obviously, I just panic when I am with them all. I can deal with individuals, but I can't handle the whole lot – it's just too much for me.

We had decided that we were not going to have a honeymoon straightaway, mainly because we had spent all our savings on the wedding. Anyway, we went away often enough on holiday and our regular trips to Spain to visit Angel Eyes' family counted as holidays to me. I had planned a trip to Rome for Angel Eyes, as he had wonderful memories of the city from a visit there when he was younger. I saved money from the next few jobs I took and I booked us a long weekend in Rome: it was my Christmas present to him.

Laura, who was the manager at Pineapple at the time, had just been to Rome with a couple of friends and had stayed at a wonderful apartment right in the centre of the city. I got all the details from her and booked it for me and Angel Eyes. We planned to go in April and before I knew it, Christmas was on our doorstep. I couldn't wait to give him the tickets, as I knew he really wanted to go. He loved the present and I got a lot of brownie points for it.

Even though it was only four days, as with any major city I knew it would be a bloody expensive trip, so all the extra work that I did outside Pineapple went into the Rome pot. We went to Rome on the weekend after my birthday. When we arrived, the weather was gorgeous and it was very romantic. I always feel very comfortable in Italy, particularly Rome,

and it makes life so much easier when you speak the language. The apartment was absolutely stunning – it was just by the big flower market at Campo dei Fiori and the smell of all the flowers was intoxicating.

I was busy thinking about how relaxing the holiday was going to be when my phone rang – and my life took another turn.

23
Celebrity Circus

Let me backtrack a bit. About a month before the holiday, I got a message from someone asking if I would be interested in being a judge on an American TV show called *Celebrity Circus*. Now this message came via Facebook, with a private email address, no sign of a production company anywhere, so I ignored it. I thought they would have contacted the production company or Sky in the UK to get my details, if they were serious.

A week later, I got another message via Facebook, with a bit more information about the new show; it was going to be filmed in Los Angeles and would air on NBC. I decided to ignore it.

When the third message arrived with a contact number, I thought I would ring this person and tell them to stop being an idiot; I wasn't going to be fooled by their prank. I got on the phone, ready for an argument and as soon as they picked up, I went straight in before they had a chance to take a breath. 'Why do you keep sending me messages on

Facebook? Why are you bothering me? What is your problem?'

I could not see how it could be a serious approach as there was no sign of a company email address or number. When I stopped speaking, the man at the other end explained that he was an independent casting agent working with an independent production company. He had seen a very short clip on YouTube of my appearance on *Cirque de Celebrité*. He said he thought I would be perfect for the show, but they would need to see more material.

It's amazing how you can start to melt when someone begins to butter you up. So, now I believed him and he said he wanted me to send him a short showreel for the American producers to see. I said I could do that, no problem. In the back of my mind, I wondered how I would do it as I had no money for a showreel and I did not want to take it out of the Rome budget. But once a dancer, always a dancer – whenever anyone asks you to do a job, just say yes. If you can't do it, you learn how to do it.

We ended the conversation with my promising to get the showreel sent straight over to him. Fortunately for me, I had a friend who worked in an editing suite, who very kindly took the time to cut a showreel for me. Once that was done, I emailed it straight across to America.

Suddenly I was consumed with what I had originally taken for a very boring prank. I thought it would be so great to go over to America and work on a big TV show. You always hear stories of the big salaries American TV stars are paid. Not that I was any kind of star, but who knows? Maybe this was going to be my lucky break. I was also looking forward to the weather as well – sun all year round!

THE WORST thing about waiting to hear from them again was the time difference between the UK and LA – I think our morning is their night. Anyway, three days after I sent off my showreel, I got a text message at about two or three in the morning. It said that the producers loved the showreel and they would like to do a conference call with me. You can imagine how excited I was.

They wanted to do the conference call on a Friday, which was three days after the text. I spent the three days in dreamland – if I got the job, they would get me a working visa. I had not thought of working in America before – and why would I, when I could not work there? The channel would take care of this and I would not have to arrange anything myself.

On the Friday morning, I spoke to the producers and that afternoon, Angel Eyes and I flew off to Rome for our delayed honeymoon. The phone meeting was great – they loved me. At least, I think they did – you can't always tell with Americans. They are always so positive – living the dream.

On our first evening in Rome I was preparing a romantic meal of pasta when the phone rang: it was Ashton, my American contact. The producers had liked me and wanted to offer me the job – they would need to see me in America in two weeks. As you can imagine, I was beside myself.

Ashton said he was going to send me an email of some information that they needed before I could apply for a visa. It was not the easy process I had imagined: I would first need to be cleared by AFTRA, the American Federation of Television and Radio Artists. I would need to prove that I was unique and that there was no-one in America who could do what I was being hired to do, as they would not just give the job to a foreigner. I had to gather news articles to show that I had some kind of status in the relevant area of work; I also needed letters of recommendation from people of standing in the entertainment industry stating I was a unique talent. All these documents had to be prepared and sent off in the next 24 hours.

I WENT from being elated to totally panic-stricken. It was night-time in Rome and I did not have a computer with me. I was not sure that there would be enough material available to support my application, despite the shows I had worked on in the UK. It was also the weekend – how was I going to get these letters of recommendation that they needed?

Once it really dawned on me what I would have to do, my heart sank. I thought of saying 'Forget it' – it seemed like an impossible task. I did not know where to begin, but in my heart of hearts, I knew I had to at least try. But this was my romantic gift to Angel Eyes – four days of 'us' time, something we had both been looking forward to. I knew Angel Eyes was pleased that we could spend time together, just the two of us, as he worked so incredibly hard most of the time.

Angel Eyes had been watching me on the phone and had seen the change from elation to tears in my eyes. I explained to him that it was not going to happen – it was just not worth it, and impossible. I thought he would agree – the time difference, in Rome, at the weekend – if we were at home, we might have a slim chance of getting it together. But I was wrong on all counts: he was having none of it.

He said, 'Right, let's make this happen.' And to my surprise, that's what we did. I made sure we had the romantic meal on the Friday night and the next day we were up, bright and breezy, in search of the nearest internet cafe to get Mission Impossible underway, with no sign of Tom Cruise.

I think there is a reason for everything – why did I speak Italian? It was surely for this day, for this Mission Impossible. We found an internet cafe that was supposed to open at 10am. Was it? Was it Mozzarella! No. Someone eventually arrived at 11am, by which time there was steam coming out of my ass. I wanted to bite his head off, but I thought it was the wrong attitude to have, in case I needed him, and I was right – I *did* need him. After I paid a euro for an hour, I got online to a barrage of about 10 emails that listed all the information they would need in America, which included a visa application form and I started to see stars. I don't know what I would have done without Angel Eyes – he took over and went through each email, one at a time.

I got in touch with my friend Caleb in London, who always helped me out whenever I needed to find anything online. He's a bit of a computer whizzkid and can usually do whatever I ask him to do in seconds, even though I might have spent a day trying to do it myself. He managed to find enough relevant newspaper articles and also sent emails to people like Richard Woolfe at Sky, Emma (Bunton, that is), Debbie Moore at Pineapple, who all wrote letters of recommendation for me.

Next was the visa application, which even at home would have been tough. The scan of my passport was the easy bit – I could do that there and then and fax it to America. But they also needed a copy of my old passport, because they needed proof of my previous working visa, which I had while dancing with the Spice Girls. The only person who could help out with that one was Piero, who had keys to my flat back in London.

Of course, when I tried to get hold of him he was unobtainable and his phone was off. I needed to get the information that day, so that the Americans would have it in the morning, which would be night-time in Europe.

While waiting to hear from Piero, we got on with what we could. Caleb had sorted out the letters and news articles, and I filled in as much of the visa application form as I could manage, leaving off every five minutes to call Piero.

Then there was the contract – this was not like the contracts in the UK, when I would sign up for the duration of the season. Apparently it is quite common in the States to sign people for up to seven years in case the show is a hit – they then have you tied in. The fee they offered would increase by a certain percentage each year that the show ran.

The money was not bad – it was a lot more than I had earned for the shows in the UK, so without consulting anyone I signed. Looking back, it was a silly thing to do but I had no agent for TV work and time was of the essence.

Finally I got hold of Piero and explained that I needed him to get my old passport scanned and emailed to me. I reached him at 7pm UK time, which was 8pm in Italy. The internet cafe shut at nine (yes, we had spent the full first day of our romantic break sitting in an internet cafe in Rome). Piero had an hour to get to my flat, find my old passport, scan it and then email it to me. You can imagine by this time I was breathing into a paper bag. I can't tell you how amazing Angel Eyes was that day; I was getting myself into a state and bit his head off at every turn – I don't know how he managed to stay so calm.

Nine o'clock arrived and still no email from Piero. The guy in the internet shop was ready to shut up and he wasn't impressed by my begging and explanations. It was only the money that talked – I felt bad that I had to spend 50 euros of our holiday money to keep the internet cafe open until I received the scan of my old passport from Piero.

The email from Piero arrived about half past nine and we put everything together and sent it to America. I can honestly say it was one of the most stressful days of my life. Once it was done, Angel Eyes and I went for a pizza – it was all we could afford then. I felt very guilty that we had spent the whole day sorting out my life, when this weekend was my gift to him. If you have ever really loved someone, there are moments when you look at them and realise how lucky you are to have someone so wonderful in your life – this was definitely one of those moments. I looked at him and thought, 'I love you'. I wanted to apologise to him for ruining our holiday as I started to say, 'I'm sorry', he stopped me and told me it had been one of the best days with me. He had never felt so close to me and felt that I depended on him.

WE HAD one day to cram in everything that Angel Eyes wanted to see and do in Rome. Even though I hated walking around and the historical sites really bored the tits off me, there was no way I could moan about anything after all that he had done for me.

We flew back to the UK on the Monday and on the Tuesday, I heard from America. All the information I had sent was correct and fine, and they would give all the papers to their lawyers to check.

I did not have time to apply for a working visa for America from the UK because I had to be in the States for meetings before I started work, which was just over a week away. The plan was that, while I was there, I could fly to Canada to pick up my visa. This worried me a lot, as there was still no guarantee that I would get the visa. As you know, I hate to fly, so I was not best pleased at the thought of having to take yet another flight – it was enough to make me consider not going. Can you believe it?

But I had my meetings in America, so I went to Canada to collect my visa and started on *Circus Celebrity*. I had a lovely apartment on Sunset & Vine, and outside the apartment was the Walk of Fame. I got a car, which is pretty much necessary in LA: no-one walks anywhere, and they really do everything bigger and better out there. I was not in a tent in a windy field, for starters – I was at the CBS studios, although the channel was NBC. I think some of *Will & Grace* was filmed there, so that was very exciting. My dressing room was not a portaloo without the loo – I had a Winnebago the size of a three-bedroom detached. I had a personal assistant, which I found very strange. It seems to be a normal thing in America, when you work on these shows.

I didn't really know what to do with mine – I wasn't very comfortable asking him to do everything for me, so I ended up telling him that I didn't really need him. This upset him a bit – I did not realise that this meant I was putting him out of a job. I didn't want to do that, so I had no choice but to send him on all my little errands. It's amazing how quickly you can change and get used to things.

I was out there for seven weeks, and I spent the first three weeks on my own, but Angel Eyes came out to join me for the last month. I suppose all of his hard work paid off really, didn't it? He didn't get his four days in Rome, but he did get a month in LA.

Now, how cushy was this? I only worked one day a week! The show was filmed on Tuesdays and aired on Wednesdays. It was definitely up there as one of the best jobs I had ever done. There was a beautiful pool in the apartment block and a gym. We would drive down to Venice – not Venice, Italy, of course, but Venice Beach. I was on a paid holiday!

The month together in LA brought Angel Eyes and me even closer together, saccharine and sickly as it may sound. I suppose life is more romantic on holiday and we were on an extended holiday away from home; we had had some really wonderful times. As for my big break in America, although the show was not a flop, it was not a massive hit either. They were very clear when we got to the end that there would not be another season. That was the end of my seven-year contract in America.

They did not use a female ringmaster for the show – our ringmaster was Joey Fatone from *NSYNC, Justin Timberlake's group. Joey was great, a real laugh. He was the only one I was allowed to speak to. In the UK we could speak to all the contestants on the show, but in America we were contractually banned from speaking to or fraternising with any of the contestants, so I didn't really build a relationship with any of them.

Dress rehearsals usually lasted a couple of hours and we were allowed to speak to the contestants then, so long as there was a representative from the station on hand. So my assistant was not just an assistant, he was also a spy, to make sure I didn't collude with Rachel Hunter, Stacey Dash or Antonio Sabato Jr.

Blu Cantrell was out of control on the show and liked to play the diva – she thought she was more special than she was. The thing is, you see, Americans always have their people with them – an agent, a publicist, a manager and a vanity – I though this was something you put your make-up in, but it's not – that's make-up and hair. And each of them has an assistant – honestly, it was silly.

Rachel Hunter did not have anyone running around after her – she was much more European in her ways, as was Antonio Sabato Jr, the first Calvin Klein model. I couldn't believe I was so close to the man who I used to have my underwear wrapped around – I mean, when I bought my briefs, he was on the packaging. I used to hate to throw it away – it seemed such a waste of a beautiful bit of card. He was still in amazing shape.

Stacey Dash, who had appeared in the film *Clueless*, was gorgeous – she looked exactly the same as she did in the movie. She was around 40 years old then, and was around 30 when she appeared in *Clueless*, playing a 15-year-old. Now there is someone I would like to have around – she could be my intravenous drip.

I know it was not strictly a holiday, although it felt like one, and normally I am ready to come home after a couple of weeks. I could have quite happily stayed longer in LA after the show ended, living the high life – I was having such a good time with Angel Eyes. But obviously we couldn't afford to do that, and Angel Eyes had to get back to work in London. Now that my seven-year contract was over, I had no choice but return to Pineapple.

24
Thirty . . . Forty

A week later, and I had slipped back into my routine – it was like America had never happened. There was a lot to get my teeth into back at Pineapple. The decorators were in the building for a revamp of the reception area, a new office and reception counter – I was busy artistically directing the lot.

As you can imagine, we were beside ourselves when we got wind of the fact that the production company that rented the top floor at Pineapple might be moving across the road. At this time, the whole of the area was being regenerated and the landlords owned pretty much all of Covent Garden. There was no way we were going to have them rent out the top floor to anyone else. At that point the studios were busier than ever.

The number of entertainment and dance shows – *Pop Idol*, *Strictly Dance Fever*, *X Factor*, *Strictly Come Dancing* – had contributed over the years to the popularity of the studios. People realised, watching the shows, that they too had a chance at the dream and the more skills they had, the better their chances. There are few pop stars nowadays who aren't knocking out a dance routine. With over 230 classes a week, in over 40 styles, Pineapple was seen as the perfect place. It is the biggest dance studio in Europe and the best by far.

What we really needed was a studio just for private hire – West End shows or pop acts who would like to rehearse after six o'clock. The studios were full after 6pm every day, and many of the dance and singing shows wanted rehearsal space in the evenings as well as during the daytime. If Pineapple could take over the top floor of the building in Langley Street, this would solve the problem straightaway.

In my mind I had already booked people in for the next year, but once again I was running before I could walk, or jumping before I could kick. Although the whisper I heard was true (upstairs wanted to move out), the fact was that they couldn't move when they wanted to because of a delay in repairs to the building they were moving into. The builders were not coming in on time – isn't that always the way? I was really looking forward to the builders coming in, making them cups of tea and helping them with their spirit levels.

It was not as if I did not have enough to get on with, being an artistic director. There was always a situation to resolve, or in my case, a show to do. The fact was that the studios were coming up to 30 years, and I was coming up to 40 – gasp! Now these were two big occasions that we had to celebrate. We were definitely planning a thirtieth for Pineapple, but I wasn't sure that I wanted to celebrate my birthday. It wasn't that I minded turning 40, I just didn't know where I would find the time to celebrate. Along with all my other roles, I was also a starmaker or dream breaker, as the song went in *Fame*.

As I've said, most jobs came through Pineapple, either for presenters or dancers and choreographers. We got wind of things early because the studios would be booked before any announcements were made and I would usually be asked for recommendations. I don't suppose that's why all the dancers complimented me constantly and told me I looked gorgeous when I looked like crap but if it was, it kept me happy.

I haven't told you, have I, that I was once a dance agent? After about five years of working at Pineapple, I was always asked about dancers and choreographers for shows and events, and I thought I could make a little business out of it. So, I went part-time at Pineapple and started Edit Agency.

It did not take long for word to get around, and all the dancers brought in CVs and photographs. I did not want to take on hundreds of people and then not get anyone work, which a lot of agencies did. After taking them on, they would try and get dancers to pay to be included in a casting book. Those books were a waste of time and a bit of a con – I never agreed to any of them. A good agent should be able to get you work based on your talent and their recommendation alone.

On the first day I sat there waiting for the phone to ring. I had let my contacts know about my new venture, but I wasn't prepared to beg for anything; I didn't think it was a good look for an agent either. I really felt I could contribute to the dancers more than anything, that I was on their side. It was a sideline for me, but I wanted to do it right and

support the dancers. As a dancer I was always sick of waiting for money from my agent: I could wait up to three months for payment, by which time that money was already used, so I was always living on an overdraft if I didn't have a regular job like a tour or a show.

It was a Catch-22 situation – you didn't want to annoy the agent by asking for your money, and you didn't want to risk not being put forward for a job that was not out there on the open market. It makes me angry that there was not a single agent who did not take longer than necessary to pay their dancers.

After a few months Edit took off, and we got some good jobs. I provided dancers and choreographers for a Will Young tour, two large Tesco commercials, Kylie, MTV, MoBo's, and many more. I almost always got the money for the jobs within a month and as soon as this arrived, I would pay the money directly into the dancers' accounts. I took a commission, but I did not hold on to their money: I realised that during all those years of waiting and lying, agents who claimed they had not received the money had no concern for their dancers' welfare.

The agency lasted for almost two years before it came to an end. It was doing well and gave me a comfortable living, but I was just the mouthpiece, the one with all the contacts. People were comfortable with me and my recommendations: they could save on castings because I provided exactly what they asked for and I had a good reputation.

When my business partner Jack (who was also a friend of mine) decided he wanted to go travelling, I felt it was something I could not carry on with on my own. There was no way I would be taking care of invoices and VAT, the things I hated most. The thought of that took the enjoyment out of running the agency. I could have hired someone else, but we had worked so well together, I knew it would not be the same. I knew I could trust this person to make sure the dancers always came first in our decisions. I had spoken to more administratively minded people to come into the company, but they all talked about holding on to the money to make interest. So I decided Edit would have to come to an end – I did not like the greed that I saw when I discussed it with the others.

I think Pineapple was happy about this as I returned to work full-time at the studios: I went straight back in and it was full-on. As soon as I started back at the studios, I went immediately into the 30-year celebrations.

THERE WERE many things planned and Debbie initially decided that instead of one big party, she would host 12 lunches or dinners at the Ivy Club in the Library. It's not really a library, it's a private room on the second floor that holds up to 14 people.

We went through a list of people who had been a part of Pineapple over the last 30 years. They did not necessarily have to be a teacher or someone who worked at the studios – they could be a business friend, or a journalist who had been supportive of Pineapple over the years. We decided mid-week was best for these get-togethers as people were usually out of town on Friday evenings.

We had some wonderful dinners, with guests including Twiggy, Sir Michael Parkinson, Christopher Biggins and

Me and the fabulous Debbie Moore OBE at
Pineapple's 30th Birthday Party.

Cleo Rocos. Actually, Cleo and I were invited to every dinner
– I think we were the cabaret, meant to keep the spirits high.
We also invited people who might be potential clients at
Pineapple, so as well as being a celebration, it was a very
clever PR stunt.

Sometimes we had repeat offenders – I mean guests – and
Debbie would always hold court. After the starters, you
would hear the clink of glass being tapped with a knife.
Everyone would look up ready to raise cheers, but it was
Debbie about to relate the story of Pineapple. The dinners
were themed 'Because of You', which was quite funny some-
times as the guest of honour might never have visited
Pineapple. After a few dinners, Cleo and I could repeat the

speech, word for word. Although the plan was for one event a month, sometimes we had two.

I'll make it quick – it would start like this: 'When I was 15, I won a modelling competition for *Honey Magazine*.' Remember, this will be brief – she went to New York, met the Beatles, came back, got married; he left her when she was 19. After a year of weeping on the Moors where she lived, she came to the Big Smoke and modelled for a bit. She developed an underactive thyroid and put on weight, and visited a homeopath who recommended dance as the perfect remedy. She started dancing at the Dance Centre, which is now The Sanctuary spa in Floral Street, in Covent Garden. She lost the weight from the thyroid problem and went back to modelling. As you can imagine, she was devastated when the Dance Centre closed with only a week's notice. The dancers would have been out on the street, so Debbie started a petition, got the numbers of all the dancers, but it happened anyway and the Dance Centre closed down.

Being the determined woman she was at that time, she mortgaged her house and found an empty building in Covent Garden. No-one wanted to be in the old fruit market which had moved out to Vauxhall, so she was able to get a good deal on the building. Once they left there were only derelict warehouses – there were no shops or many businesses in the area. If you want to know why it is called Pineapple Dance Studios, it is because the building used to be an old pineapple warehouse.

She took the first floor and the basement, and over the next 30 years continued to take over other floors of the building. This was the speech each time and it would end, 'because of you and your support', to the guest of honour, whatever their role. It worked fantastically – it was a very clever way of celebrating at the time. The only thing it was not good for was the waistline: I could never resist and always took all three courses. It just meant I had to walk home faster to burn it all off.

I THINK once you are past 35, you tend to retain a little bit more weight than you are used to, and I was no longer 35. My 40th birthday was getting close and I had already decided I would not have a big hoo-ha. I just wanted to celebrate with my close friends and family, on two separate occasions. You know I can't relax when all the family is together – it's not their fault, it's just me. I wanted a quiet venue that would not cost a fortune; I remembered that while we were looking for a venue for the wedding, we had found a bar in Soho called The Edge. They would waive a hire fee in exchange for a certain amount at the bar. That was when I could have done with my family on hand – they would have smashed the bar bill in one round. But I always had Laura to count on, the lovely manager of Pineapple Dance Studios. She could always drink a shot or two, or three, or four.

Jason was not going to be much help as he was teetotal, but there were a few other friends I knew I could rely on. If not, I would just have to get the credit card out – it was one of the big birthdays, after all. Although apparently 40 is now the new 30, with my regime and body maintenance it could even be the new 20 for me – or maybe 25, with that little bit of back fat. I know what you're thinking, there's nothing to you, but when you are used to one weight and you suddenly put on a stone between 35 and 40, it doesn't help to be surrounded by 20-year-olds who remind you of how you used to look, as hot as a stripper in the Sahara.

I thought I was not having a mid-life crisis. You hear a lot about straight men having affairs and going to lap-dancing clubs wearing skinny jeans and open-necked shirts. Hang on, that sounds like me! Maybe I was having one after all. As for wanting a big fast car, I absolutely did, not that I ever drove anywhere. I had never owned a new car, and always had my sister Kelly's leftovers. My first car was an orange-red Ford Fiesta, then a Volvo. After the Volvo, I had a Ford Fiesta XR2i – black, with blue speed stripes down the sides. I know what you're thinking – it's quite boy racer. I do get full of testosterone driving around London, leaning on the horn, gesticulating at the men in their white vans. Then I had a white Escort XR3i 1.6, with a spoiler on the back and – wait for it – a bass drum in the boot.

Surprise you? Yes, I surprise myself sometimes. Anyway, I really wanted a brand-new nice car. A few years earlier I house-sat and car-sat for Piero while he was on holiday. He had done quite well for himself: he and his partner had lovely cars and while they were away, I had to make sure the battery did not go flat on the car. That's when I took out his convert-ible Jag and it felt nice, driving a quality car.

I was more than happy with my hand-me-downs before, but you don't know what something is like until you try it. Now I knew what it was like, I had set myself a target that by the time I was 40 I wanted a proper car, a man's car. I didn't know how I was going to get it, but that was what I wanted.

I treated myself to a new car; it wasn't quite the Jag I wanted, but it was brand new, and I managed to get £2,000 off the price by scrapping my old car, which was more than 10 years old. I say I got it for myself, but actually Angel Eyes paid half. So we got ourselves – wait for it, drum roll – a brand-new black, central-locking Hyundai i10, with CD and radio. Not quite the manly Jag that I wanted, but it was my first-ever new car. It works out very good for parking – I think it could fit inside a Mini. We always travel light, and it's usually just the two of us, and in the back there is only room for a small child. Angel Eyes brings this up in conversation now and then, but I still don't know if we're ready for kids even though we're married. Where would we put them in a one-bedroom? He can keep thinking on that one.

ON THE night of my fortieth I left work with Laura and Caleb, who also worked at Pineapple with me, and we walked up to Soho to The Edge. We arrived an hour before everyone and the evening was lovely. The room was the perfect size, and there was a white piano in the corner, and I played a bit of chopsticks. I thought I would let down what was left of my hair and go over my two-glass quota of rosé – I got those down me before anyone arrived. The first to arrive after us was Angel Eyes, who was quite surprised to see me on my third glass of rosé. He seemed to find it funny, as he had never seen me go beyond my quota.

It did not make it any easier reaching 40 and having a toy boy. Did I mention he is eight years younger than me? I don't think the age difference is too obvious. Next, Carmine arrived with some balloons – don't ask me why the balloons. Then Jason, and Duncan James, from Blue, and the last of my friends to arrive was Emma. She's much better with time-keeping now she is a mum, but she used to be the last to turn up anywhere. She came with her gorgeous beau, Jade.

Someone jumped on the old joanna and there were a few songs, very spicy and blue, if you know what I mean. I did my version of Mistoffeles, which you can imagine was one big spit, after my intake of rosé. Although I did not have my Lycra or tail on, I still ended up on top of the piano hissing and purring.

It was not a very late night, but it was a wonderful evening, looking around at my few but very close friends. As always, the evening ended with me and Angel Eyes carrying Laura and Caleb out. We managed to get Laura on a night bus and as Caleb was going from Waterloo, we half-carried, half-dragged him across the bridge. We left him on his merry way to catch a train, even though we offered to put him up. He insisted he was quite sober and could make his own way home. I wasn't going to argue as my arms were shot after the drag across the bridge. They survived, slightly the worse for wear the next day at work, but somehow they both made it in. What a night!

25

TVWs

Back at Pineapple we got word that the company on the top floor would definitely be moving out within the next six months, which was great news for us as there were more demands for hire space. There seemed to be more and more dance shows and we were always short of space to accommodate them.

I found the meetings with architects very boring – it was all condensation and insulation, and only the cute junior architect kept my interest up. I was much happier being on reception – the conversation there stimulated me more. It could be superficial sometimes, but better than chatting with architects.

After a particularly boring meeting, Luke, who I worked with, told me I had a call from the BBC. I called them back and when I got through someone explained that they were bringing *So You Think You Can Dance* to the UK. This was a popular show in America and I had watched it religiously when I was in LA working on *Celebrity Circus*. It was an amazing show that I found very inspirational; every time I watched it, I wanted to dance. It ran for about 10 weeks and was open to professional and non-professional dancers. Most of the finalists were professionals, and the prize was $100,000 and an apartment in New York, if I remember correctly.

SYTYCD showed off the versatility of the dancers, who went easily from Argentinian tango to hip hop, from contemporary to lyrical, and from musical theatre to classical ballet. I remember one show with a dancer who was truly breathtaking and he seemed to master every style of dance that he performed. It was a show that was necessary as new dancers in the industry seemed to be focussing on one style only, mainly hip hop and street dance. There is obviously a technique to it, but it does not take as much training as classical ballet, or require as much technique as lyrical jazz. It is really just a quick fix – it will get you one type of job, but it will limit you as a dancer.

That's why I thought *SYTYCD* was so important in educating young dancers that they were limiting their potential by focussing on one style only. When they told me at the BBC that they were looking for judges and that they wanted to see my showreel, I was so excited. Of all the judging jobs I had done on TV, if there was one that I knew I would be right for, it was this one.

It was such perfect timing for me – I was mature enough at 40, and I felt I was more than qualified. I had never limited myself as a dancer and I had tried every style. I felt I had mastered many in my career; without blowing my own trumpet, I knew there was little I did not know about what was current in dance. Working at Pineapple every day, I was one of the first to become aware of anything new that was break-ing through. There are many dancers with the same experi-ence and versatility as me, but what they did not have was that bird's-eye view of everything that went on. This job was meant for me – I really had something to say on *SYTYCD*.

I sent my showreel and then waited. As you already know, I'm not very good at waiting, and I could think of nothing else. I really wanted to be a part of this amazing show that I had seen in America, one that would stimulate and encour-age dancers. If it also had the same prize money, a dancer would be able to afford to attend dance college, afford to live in London, but beyond that, it was great exposure for real dancers.

The BBC had checked out my showreel online and, after a couple of days, I got an email asking me if I could recommend anyone else for the job. I must say that pissed me off, and I thought it was bloody rude, but I reminded myself – TVWs. I swallowed my pride and gave them a list of names of people I thought would be great for my job. I recommended good people, knowing that it would reflect on me; I had reached a point when I knew that if a job in this industry was meant for you, you would get it. There are no secrets in showbusiness, as I said before, and you can't keep jobs from people.

To cut a long story short, I did not get the job and as usual, I did not get a phone call telling me this. I found out from one of the people I had recommended, who got the job: a choreographer named Sisco, who was great in the role. Even though I really wanted the job, the good thing about age is that it is easier to deal with these disappointments. It teaches you to value the important and relevant things in your life and ignore the superficial things.

BACK AT the Pineapple ranch, we were still in meetings, not only with architects; I was getting excited because the builders were coming in, all hard hats and Hi-Vis jackets. That's usually enough to keep me interested.

To fit in with the regeneration going on around Covent Garden, we planned to move the shop that was next door to the corner across the road and move the Pineapple offices to the top floor of the studios, next to the new studio that we were going to build.

We had a bit of a battle on our hands, as the office team needed a certain amount of space, but I wasn't prepared to give up studio space to fit an extra desk in. We were not going to budge on studio size, and Laura and I won the battle. We managed to get exactly what we wanted and when the drawings were brought in, the studio looked amazing, with two large windows. There is nothing like daylight when you want to choreograph – a basement and strip lighting are never stimulating. The studio had to be special, as this was also going to be incorporated into the 30-year celebration.

I was already envisioning a press launch in our brand-new studio, with dancers and celebs rubbing shoulders and sipping champers. And before I could say dirty builders in concrete dust, they were in, smashing down walls, ripping out windows, and generally being very butch and builder-like. I ran around like a blue ass fly making myself busy, trying to keep a happy and harmonious work environment. I tried to appease the ballerinas, who complained of choking on cement dust, and our studio hires, who complained about the constant banging while trying to hold auditions. It's not like there was enough of me to go round to start with.

So there I was, run off my feet as usual, doing this, that and everything, when Aidan on reception shouts over with the phone in his hand, 'Louie, it's for you.'

'Who is it?'

'I don't know' – don't you just hate that, when you have to ask who it is? Don't you just do that, when you answer the phone? I know you don't do it at home, but in your place of work? I always do.

'Well, ask who it is and what they want.'

So, it's another TV exec; they're all so full of crap. The usual line, 'We think it would be a great place to do a show. You know, there's so much going on. We think we could do this, we think we could do that.' And they all get it so wrong; they have absolutely no understanding of how dance works. Why would they? I suppose, they haven't lived it like me.

You try to explain to them how it works, how the people are, what you think would be best. When I say you, I mean me. But most of them would always come back with a format they had in mind, which was all doom and gloom, totally uninspired, and not true to the world I lived in. Which most of the time is full of so much joy and happiness and amazingly inspirational people, like myself may I add. Yes, I may, it's my book – I'll add what I want.

Anyway, I pick up. 'Hello, Louie speaking, artistic director of Pineapple Dance Studios.' And off he goes; got a great idea for a show, blah blah blah, blah blah blah, blah. 'I'm only around the corner, would I be able to pop in and see you?'

I mean, really, who do these people think they are? Like they think I've got nothing to do, I'm going to drop everything because some TV exec wants to come and see me.

'Well, no, I'm sorry – I'm far too busy. Let me just check my diary.'

So I put him on hold. 'Laura! I've got another one of the TV wankers on the phone. He wants to pop in and see us; he says he's only around the corner. I told him no, I'm far too busy. I'm checking my diary. Have I got anything going on?'

'When do you ever have anything going on?'

'Laura, really. Anyone would think I stand behind you and annoy you all day.'

'You do!'

'Oh, let's have him in tomorrow, he might be cute. And you need a husband.'

'What does he sound like?'

'Educated, quite softly spoken, but to the point. I'm seeing shirt hanging out, jeans and Hush-Puppy shoes.'

'Well, I'm busy in the morning. I've got to get my things ready for a board meeting.'

'Great, let's do him at 11am.'

'Hello? Yes, I've just checked my diary – I've had a cancellation. I can do tomorrow morning at 11am. Failing that, I can do next month.'

'11 o'clock tomorrow morning, Laura.'

You see, the thing is, it's not that I think I know best but I know I do when it comes to dance. I am generalising, I know, but I have dealt with a lot of these TV people: they just want to sensationalise everything. That's some word for me to say; imagine if books were in 3D, you would need a spitguard for 'sensationalise'. Why is it that people always seem to think that tragedy and failure is far more interesting?

When I say 'people', I'm going back to TV people, I don't mean us. When I say 'us', I mean me and you.

How does it happen? I'm drifting now, but it's just come into my mind. How does it happen that some of these people manage to get jobs with great power without knowing jack shit about what the job entails?

Now, there is a casting couch that still exists – it does in showbiz. I've never been on it, my talent has always taken me through with my great backflips and my high kicks; I never had to go horizontal for anyone. Maybe it's called a casting desk, or a casting counter in the catering industry. Who knows? Anyway, my point is, just because someone has a title like TV executive or supervisor/manager, it doesn't mean they always know best.

It can be very difficult to get my point across when these people come in to see me to tell me how my industry works and that the best way to make a TV programme about it is doom gloom doom gloom doom gloom.

Now, I said it can be difficult to get my point across, but after seeing so many, at the end of their schpiel, sometimes I would be so incensed I would just tell them it was a pile of crap and we weren't interested. I'd watch their face collapse in horror and absolute disbelief that I could be so cutting and to the point. It is very easy to be cutting and to the point when you have been a dancer; you get a lot of disappointment and cutting comments, but you still have to leave high-kicking with a smile on your face.

And that's exactly what I would do after one of these meetings; I'd get up, smile, pirouette, high-kick and make my exit, just because I could and it really made me laugh. Because they just didn't get it!

I knew that they would be trying to work out what just happened. And if they didn't get what just happened, then they didn't get me, they didn't get Pineapple, and they didn't get this industry. It is full of passionate, dedicated, crazy people. When I say 'crazy', I don't mean sectionable crazy – I just mean people who can laugh at themselves and not take life too seriously. Because in this industry you don't know where you're going to be from one day to the next, or when your life is going to change. And it can happen as quick as lightning, I can tell you that for a fact.

So there we were, me and Laura, just gone to get our coffees. Coffees only in the winter, and mine is always decaf – I can't do stimulants. Honestly, caffeine would get me palpitating and I'd have a panic attack, unless they are about six foot two, Spanish, and stacked. It's my husband I'm talking about. That's the only stimulant I would have and it's the only one I need. I always have an almond croissant as well with my coffee, just to get me through until lunchtime.

It's five to 11. Now, I'm an absolute stickler for punctuality. So we have the TV guy coming in at 11 o'clock and I'm wolfing down my croissant because I have to clean my teeth before he arrives. Regardless of whether he is going to be as dull as dishwater, I still like to present myself with nice smelling breath. If you're in close proximity to someone and they have a bit of hali, get a tongue scraper – that's what you need for hali.

IT'S ONE minute past 11, and he's not here. My time is precious, my time is costly, and I don't like waiting when I have so much to do. 'Haven't I, Laura?'

'Yeah, right, whatever.'

At five past 11, I make it very clear to Aidan that if anyone comes in now, I will be in a meeting.

Ten past 11, 'Louie, there's someone here to see you.'

'Great, thanks, Aidan.' You just can't get the staff, can you?

We have blinds in the office so we have a little peek through. I know he's late, but if he's cute we'll speak to him. I was right – Hush-Puppy shoes, always a worry. History teachers and wankers, but his saving grace is that he has salt and pepper hair, which Laura loves. And by the looks of it, quite a nice ass – not that I'm interested, I'm married. I'm just thinking of Laura.

By this time Laura has almost smashed her head through the window. You only have to mention salt and pepper to her and she is like a woman possessed. I'm just praying he doesn't have blue eyes, otherwise I will have to do all the talking while she sits and salivates.

Well, it's lucky I can talk the leg off a chair, isn't it? He's got blue eyes like the warm waters of the Med; you just want to dive in and float around. Now, if it wasn't for the fact that Laura wanted to pant over him, I would have told him that he had missed his chance. If someone can't turn up on time for the first meeting then it's a sign of bad things to come, but like I said, I'm not thinking about me, I'm thinking about Laura. I'm not even looking at his tight, peachy rear in the white jeans he is wearing.

So we go upstairs to the cafe and sit down. Well, I'm sorry, I've got Laura sitting there panting and I've just skipped a heartbeat. Now, I don't mean to be crude or graphic, but there are some things that you can't ignore or you can't help but look at.

When he sat down he had the biggest packet I had seen in a long time. And when I say 'packet' I don't need to explain, do I? Before I knew it, I said, 'My God, you've got a big packet!' And without missing a beat, he replied, 'Yes, I've got huge balls.'

By this time Laura had collapsed next to me and I don't even need to hear what he's got to say. I'm thinking he can film what he likes, when he likes, how he likes.

When I say he, Jonathan Stadlen is his name, which later becomes 'Straddle-him', but you will have to wait for that.

I must not be sidetracked, I must hear him out – concentrate, concentrate, concentrate! By this time I was wondering whether or not they had given me a decaf. I'm contained, I'm controlled, I'm together.

And what is this I'm hearing? Joyful, positive, laughter, true representation – can this man really be from TV? Handsome, charming, a tight ass and big balls. 'Yes, yes, *yes!*' I don't know where it came from, I was like Meg Ryan in *When Harry Met Sally*.

And that is how it all started – the wonderful world of Sky1's *Pineapple Dance Studios*.

26
Straddle-him

Well, believe it or not (believe it), for someone who arrived late for their first meeting, Jonathan Stadlen ('Straddle-him') took no time in getting back to us. Within one hour of his leaving, he was on the phone telling me how he would like to come around and do a taster.

Once again my heart skipped a beat at the thought of him having a nibble. Well, I can tell you, Laura and I were already buttered and ready for the filling; we were more than happy for him to slip between our slices.

But it wasn't that kind of tasting at all. What he meant was – this is what they do in TV – he wanted to come back with a little camera and just film around the studios to get the ambience and the feeling. He said it would only take about an hour, and what they do is edit it down to about five minutes and take it around the TV channels and see who wants to put it on.

You can imagine by now I had already lost interest – I was still thinking about the sandwich. I regained enthusiasm when he mentioned that he would like me to lead this tour of the studio, something I do all the time. I said of course, no problem at all.

'Great, I'll be there tomorrow. Is midday good?'

You see, being a morning person, I am an early riser. I'm a creature of habit – I get up bright and breezy. Now, I don't shower in the morning, I'll always have a hot bubble bath at night. I have my four egg whites with my soya milk and a banana, and my fish oil tablets, because it's good for the brain, apparently, and keeps you lubricated. I scrape my tongue and clean my teeth, put my gym clothes on with my daywear in the man bag, which would have been prepared the night before. Oh, I forgot, I always have a spray of deodorant as well – there's nothing worse than Bobby Orange (BO) in the morning. I find it inexcusable, there is just no need.

I'll walk to the gym, which is about a mile and a half, and that's my cardio. I can't do running machines, they are boring and I can't do sweating. I spend about an hour in the gym, 45 minutes of that gossiping with the gays and the girls, and every now and then the guys. Five-minute workout, five-minute shower, and then I walk to work, which is about five minutes away.

Now, this is all done by nine o'clock. My point is, this is why midday meetings, especially anything on camera, are always good for me. The mind and body might be awake, but there's nothing you can do with puffy eyes – that's just time, isn't it? So, by midday I'm suitably pleasing on the eye. So I said, 'Yes, midday is fine, see you then, blue eyes.'

I didn't give him a chance to respond to that, I just put the phone down. I wanted to see how he would react to me the next day; I wanted to see how far I could push this blue-eyed boy with the peachy rear. Married with three kids, yes, I know, and I'm married and I'm very happy, but it's the little things in life that get you through the day, isn't it?

I didn't know whether or not to tell Laura that he would be coming in the next day, especially after our last encounter. What with her panting and salivating – no, actually, I had best tell her. We don't want another episode like that. All that drool could create a Health & Safety issue.

'Laura, he's coming in tomorrow at midday.'

'Who?'

'Straddle-him.'

'Who?'

'Straddle-him! Salt and pepper, blue eyes like the warm waters of the Med.'

'No!'

'Yes, love, he's coming to film! He wants to do a taster.'

'A *what*?'

'A taster. I know, I thought exactly the same.'

'What do you mean, what's a taster?'

'My understanding, from what he said, is that he wants to come and film me. You haven't got a chance, darling – I know he's married with three kids, but I've won him over. It's my low vee tees and my big tits, it will always work.'

'Oh shut up, what is he doing? Come on! What am I gonna wear?'

'You don't have to worry. I can see he's only got eyes for me. No, what he wants to do is, he wants to come in, he wants me to give him a tour, the usual. You know what we do when people come in – well, me. But you're right, Laura, what are you going to wear?'

'Do you think I should wear my hairpiece?'

'It depends how far you think you're going to get. I think it can be a bit of a worry for straight men: they think they've picked up one thing and by the time they get you home, if you're that kind of girl, and I'm not saying you are. But, for those who are, I mean, really. So, you take off your hair, you take off your make-up, you take your chicken filets out and you have no tits or you take your Wonderbra off and they are hanging down to your waist. You then take your six-inch heels off and you look like a reject from the Yellow Brick Road that the Wicked Witch of the East has cast a spell on. Go natural like me, it always works.'

'You mean I should look like a pig, so that you get all the attention?'

'Laura, really!'

'Yeah, really.'

'Whatever, darling, it's at 12 o'clock tomorrow. Do what you have to do, darling. I have to go and artistic direct around this studio.'

NEXT DAY

'Ooooh, you've gone all out today, haven't you? What is this, a tit competition?'

'No, I always wear this.'

'Yeah, right – when you're going out on the pull! So, do you want to come and do this tour with me and Straddle-him?'

'No, no, it's fine. You do it, because you do it best.'

'Alright, I'll bring him here first.'

'No, don't.'

'Why? You've got all dressed up.'

'No, I'm going out with the girls tonight, that's why I got all dressed up.'

'Right.'

'I'm just praying for Straddle-him's sake that he's not late. Honestly, once is really hard for me to forgive, but I can just about do it. There's no second time around for me, I'm sorry. I'm far too busy pretending I'm far more important than I really am.'

So, here we go. Five to 12 – do I want him to be late so we can have our first tiff? No, I don't actually, I have to be somewhere at one, and that's all I can give him. He said it would only take an hour.

Five, four, three, two, 'Hello, Louie.'

Oh, just on the strike of 12 – no lovers' tiff this time.

'So, what is it exactly you would like me to do? Tell me where you want to start and how we're going to do this.' I was thinking in my mind, 'When you're married with three kids and obviously smitten by me.' See, I can't help it – sometimes these things just happen in my mind. You know when you're a kid and someone says don't do something and you just do it?

Now, I don't have Tourettes but I imagine it must be like this, sometimes you just want to say it. Or maybe I do have a form of it and it just hasn't been diagnosed. When I say 'it', I mean things that you shouldn't say, but it just makes me laugh to do it.

But Straddle-him seemed like the kind of guy that I could joke around like that with. Considering I mentioned his big

balls the first time we met, I just presumed that with him the sky was the limit.

So, back to my tour. He tried to tell me where he'd like to start, what he'd like to do and how he'd like to do it, but as I mentioned previously, when you don't understand something, leave it to the people who do. That was me, so I decided where we'd start, what we'd do and how we'd do it. I directed it all actually, and I never let Jonathan forget it – I always tell him that without me, he would be nothing. But we will get to that conversation later on.

27
Pineapple Chunks

So we started at the very beginning, on the four steps outside Pineapple, with me entering the reception area and giving a brief description of the people we have going through the doors and the kind of classes we have going on. I then introduced the reception staff, giving Laura a chance to compose herself before entering the office. When we went in, she looked, laughed and blushed.

I asked her once more if she wanted to join us. She seemed to have lost her tongue, and just shook her head and turned even redder.

I thought that was a good moment to exit the office and move on. As I glided up the stairs, I introduced passing dancers to my crew and elegantly manoeuvred in and out of all 11 studios, chatting and high-kicking, backflipping and spinning and generally giving Jonathan Straddle-him what I believed he wanted – me.

It was now one o'clock and his hour was up: I had to be elsewhere. I was off for lunch at the Ivy with Debbie Moore.

'Can you just do another hour? The tour was amazing, but can you introduce us to any interesting characters?'

'Darling, they don't get more interesting than me! You've had your hour, I suggest you go and make your taster tape tasty.'

'Oh, no, I didn't mean it like that. You're amazing.'

'Yes, I know.'

'No, what I mean is, when we present these kinds of things we need to show that there are a few stories to follow that would hold the public's interest, along with all the other wonderful things that go on here, like the classes and rehearsals.'

'Yeah, yeah, I've got it. What you're saying is that I'm not enough on my own. It's alright, I get it. I'm not offended, I'm a professional. Just say what you mean, like you're in love with me. Did I say that? Well, I haven't got time to do it now. I told you you've only got an hour, I have to be somewhere. Call me tomorrow at 10, and make sure it is at 10. You're lucky you got this far, darling, what with being 10 minutes late for our first meeting.'

'Yes, I know, I was just—'

'Yeah, whatever, 10 o'clock – and wear those tight white jeans.'

More interesting people, really. Well, it's not a problem at all – the place was full of them. Well, I say interesting, it all depends on what you find interesting.

Now, there's Doris: I absolutely adore her, she's so sweet. She can't remember who she is or where she is; I can't figure out how she remembers to come to her classes on Tuesdays and Thursdays, but in she comes.

'Hello, Doris, how are you?'

'Am I late?'

'No, love – your class isn't for another two hours.'

'Am I early then?'

'Yes, Doris, you're early.'

'How much is it then?'

'Have you not got your card I gave you, Doris? Remember I gave you a card, a lifelong membership?' I gave it to her last year, on her ninetieth birthday.

'What card? Do you want me to have a look?'

'It's alright, Doris, you don't have to look. I know you've got it, it's fine. Why don't you go and get changed?'

'Should I get changed then?'

'Yes, Doris, get changed.'

Well, this is the reason I love Doris. I thought only I could stop traffic leaving Pineapple. Well, I kid you not, Doris would appear from the changing room at the reception asking if her class had started. Actually asking the same questions she had asked 10 minutes earlier, but this time she had her dancing gear on.

Well, partly. From the waist up, there she was in her black ballet wrap that smelled of Rich Tea biscuits that had been dipped in tea. The reason I can be so precise about this smell is because the Rich Tea biscuits that had been dunked in tea had missed her mouth and ended up in crusty patches all over her wrap. But she wasn't stopping traffic because of this fashion faux pas, or the sweet smell of Pond's Cold Cream; I think it was more to do with the fact that she had forgotten to put her knickers on.

So there she was, standing at reception with her ballet shoes, worn-out, laddered old ballet tights and no knickers. Doris is 90, and no matter how many ballet classes you do, at 90 you can't help but have an ass like a Sharpei dog, if you have no knickers on to hold it all in. Now this was a regular occurrence, but was it interesting enough or not? I thought so.

AND THEN of course there's Andrew Stone. 'Stone, Stone, Andrew Stone.' I don't think he's ever forgiven me for beating him in *Junior Star Time* in 1985. He must have been about 14 and I was 16, there isn't a huge age gap. Although he currently confesses to being 28 and I'm 41. I don't know, you do the maths. He is the Peter Pan of pop.

Now you can take Andrew one way or the other. A complete knob, or someone who is living their dream – I'll go for the latter. His self-belief and determination, or is that delusion, is unique. He truly believes he is as talented as Justin Timberlake and that he can be as big as Robbie Williams; that he will have a number one album all over the world; that he is a God to all women. And I can't say for certain, and this is only my view, but I have a feeling he may help us out when we're busy and by us I mean 'us', gay men.

On this occasion I think I can speak on behalf of us gay men when I say that I don't think we'll ever be that busy. But hey, he is living his dream. He's not out there knocking old ladies over the head or selling crack. He's not doing any harm to anyone – well, he wasn't until this programme started. He could be regarded as a role model – don't give up on your dreams. You never know when someone is going to come knocking at your door.

Do I want to give him the chance to have his door kicked down? Should I mention him to Jonathan? Would the nation appreciate his overwhelming talent, or should I say talents? Yes, why not? He deserves another chance after *Junior Star Time*.

BUT AS I explained to Jonathan, there are many people like Andrew who come through the doors – it's the nature of the place. Now, I don't want to repeat myself, but I will. There's something for everyone and everyone for something, and we don't discriminate. It makes the world a much better place and makes for a much brighter life, believe me! All the sparkle can be blinding, I'm telling you.

I was sure that if Jonathan could get excited about Andrew, he would love Lobster Man – he was a treat for everyone. I mean, really, if you were going to be a Lord, why would you be Lord of the Lobsters? I don't think it's a very interesting shellfish, do you? You just get your claws tied up and boiled. Believe me, on more than one occasion I've wanted to tie his claws up and boil him. As I say, Lobster Man is another one of our colourful members who give Pineapple its unique character.

Well, I say member, but it's really *members* – yes, there are two of them, identical twins. I know it's hard to believe, but yes, it is true. There are two, who tried to use the same membership card – not as identical as they thought when it comes to me checking the cards on the door. Mind you, they got away with it for quite a few years. I'm in my eleventh year at Pineapple now and I don't know how long they were at it. It must be about 20 years, because I saw them here when I was rehearsing for *Bugsy Malone* when I was 14.

Every day they would come to class and they never really succeeded, but they loved it and it made them happy, and that's all that counts at the end of the day, really, isn't it? Maybe that's why he became Lord of the Lobsters – he could create his own technique, his own style – which he definitely has. When you hear him wailing his own songs in the studios, anyone would think he was being boiled because his material definitely sounds to me like a cry for help, but for some reason no-one comes running. I knew Jonathan was going to love him.

NOW, ONE thing I wasn't prepared to do, no matter how cute I found Jonathan, was to bend over backwards for him. That's another thing I've learned with my TV experiences, and in life generally: the more you give, the more someone will take, and I'm not about to do anyone's job for them. I've got enough on my plate as artistic director of the biggest dance studios in Europe without having to choreograph and direct a TV show. No, if he wants this, he'll have to come begging.

The thing is with me, I find it hard to stop myself – I can't help but give, give, give. Or is it that I'm a control freak? Well, either or; I'm not, not, *not* doing it this time. I've given him an inch – he's the one who will have to give a mile to make this happen.

'Laura, it was 10 o'clock, wasn't it?'

'What's 10 o'clock?'

'Jonathan, tomorrow morning – we said 10 o'clock, didn't we? I was too busy looking down south.'

'Yes, it was 10 o'clock.'

'Well, I'd best ring Andrew to see if he'll be around tomorrow. Well, if he's not, I'm sure he'll make himself available as soon as I mention cameras and TV show. That's if he's not on a sell-out tour in his own sitting room.'

'Hello, Pulse Films.'

'Hi, could I speak to Jonathan Straddle-him, please?'

'Jonathan who, sorry?'

'Jonathan Straddle-him.'

'Oh, you mean Stadlen?'

'No, I mean Straddle-him.'

'Ha ha' – nervous laughter from the receptionist.

'Hi, Straddle-him, it's Louie.'

'It's Stadlen.'

'I know what it is, darling, but if this is going to work you'd better get used to Straddle-him. Anyway, listen, I haven't got much time, I'm very busy. I've spoken to Andrew Stone – he can be in tomorrow about midday. Well, by the time he gets his make-up on after class, you're looking at more like two o'clock. So instead of 10, come at two tomorrow, unless you need to do any more with me.'

'Well, I thought it would be great if you were there to maybe do an introduction to Andrew, like you did yesterday ...'

'Yes, yes, fine, I know! I'll see you at two.'

THE NEXT day Jonathan arrived on time.

'Well, blow me down and pick me back up, get a load of this, Laura!'

At this point I was peering through the blinds in the office, pretending that I was busy. I was just paying Jonathan back for being late the day before. He had come with a treat – a six foot four cameraman, the spit of Johnny Depp, no word of a lie!

Well, I had my eyelash curlers out, brushed my eyebrows and was out in reception before you could have said Joe le Taxi or Vanessa Paradis.

'Oh great, Louie. I was on time today, you see?'

'You don't get points for being on time, Jonathan, but you do for bringing Johnny Depp along. Hello, Louie – nice to meet you.'

'Yeah, nice to meet you, man – Josh.'

'Now, looking at you, darling, we definitely need to get this show commissioned, don't we? We could do with you around all the time! Do you work for Pulse, Josh?'

'Yeah, yeah, yeah I do.'

'Grrrreat! Let's get this show on the road! Are there many more like this back at the office, Jonathan?'

'Haha.'

'Haha ha. Right, let's go up to the cafe. Andrew should be up there by now, unless he's still putting on his make-up. You'll see what I mean – it's quite a heavy base and he tends to forget his neck. Follow me, Josh, it's just one flight up.'

Well, shock horror – more horror than shock, there was Andrew waiting in the cafe.

'Oh, I see what you mean about the base, man.'

'I'm loving you already, Josh ... Hey Andrew, how are you, love? I didn't think you'd be on time, getting all that on your face.'

'Ha ha, stop it, Louie, what are you like?'

'Pretty hot, wouldn't you agree, Josh? Jonathan, this is Andrew, who I told you about. Jonathan has already checked you out on YouTube, the video of the photoshoot – you know, the one with the leather tassels and mesh skirt thing, whatever it was. The one where you said you were an undiscovered ready-made pop star. Well, think of Jonathan as your Christopher Columbus – you are about to be discovered.'

'Oh yeah, hi Jonathan, it's nice to meet you. If you've seen some of my stuff, then, you know ... As you can see, I'm a triple threat: I'm a musician, actor, dancer, singer, choreographer.'

'I think you've passed triplet there, darling – you're on to sextuplets. But like I said, Jonathan, you wanted people who were one-offs.'

'Yeah, I am that.'

'You certainly are, darling.'

'So Andrew, what we'd like to do is to film you singing at the piano, maybe do a bit of dancing. Explain who you are, what you're looking for.'

'You know, Andrew, just be you, darling! Come on, let's go up to studio 10, it's free for a couple of hours. We can do it there.'

It didn't take much of a push for Andrew to give Jonathan what he wanted. Before you knew it, there he was churning out his own material and telling Jonathan that the least he expected was a number one hit around the world, how much talent he had, what a hit he was with the girls and how great he was in bed.

I occasionally had to lift Jonathan's jaw off the floor – I could see he couldn't believe this was for real, that there was someone with so much self-belief and self-confidence. But I have to say he really doesn't have a bad bone in his body – Andrew, that is. He just truly believes in himself. I say believes in himself, he did once compare himself to Jesus. I suppose that was just one step too far for me, but I'm sure God will forgive him.

28

Riff-raff with a little *je ne sais quoi*

Once we finished filming with Andrew in the studio I asked Jonathan what he would do next. He explained that he would go away to edit all the footage that he had filmed over the last two days and make the five-minute taster that he had mentioned.

I could see he was getting very excited, and I don't mean his packet was getting bigger, although you would have thought it was by the way I kept gazing down south. It was obvious to me that he was aware he had just walked into something that could potentially change his life. Yes, *me*. I think he could smell the success, long before any of us.

I knew it, and he knew it. He was the one I was going to let in, after 30 years of Pineapple, to make a documentary about us. Well, once again, I say 'I'. As artistic director, I do have a lot of roles to fill but the final say would be made by the one and only DeMoore (that's what I like to call her). I suppose her real title would be Debbie Moore, OBE, icon,

Business Woman of the Year, first woman chairman on the London Stock Exchange.

But as you can imagine, for someone with so many titles to her name, she is very busy and the only respite she manages to get is when she pops off to the Ivy with me. I don't mean the restaurant, I mean the club. Let me tell you, it's very posh and star-studded. See, I never would have got in there if it wasn't for her. DeMoore, OBE, icon, is a founder member. Ooh, it's lovely, it has a glass lift, but you have to be careful with it as the doors open outwards; it's quite funny seeing celebrities and wannabes getting smacked in the face by it. The club is beautifully lit – I suppose it has to be, doesn't it, when you think of all the stars who pass through the doors? The first time I was there I saw Kate Moss before she became my NBF. You wouldn't want to light these stars badly or I'm sure they wouldn't be coming back in a hurry. In such a venue you want to look beautiful in every position – I mean wherever you're seated.

It's very art-deco inspired, with lovely sofas, wood panelling, and peanuts and olives with every drink, and you don't have to pay for them! All the staff know your name; I guess the reason being that you swipe your membership card when you enter – because not just anyone can join. You have to be nominated to become a member – I suppose that keeps the riff-raff out, doesn't it? That's why Debbie Moore was a member and not me.

Mind you, I like to look upon myself as riff-raff with a little *je ne sais quoi*. I don't know what my *je ne sais quoi* is, but neither do they at the Ivy Club and I seem to be getting away with it. Ooh, I'll tell you the best bit about it – the toilets!

No, don't get any filthy ideas. They have this hand cream by Aesop – it's an Australian brand available in Liberty's – it's fabulous, and it's not even stuck down, anyone could nick it. But I haven't; what I did instead was buy a 99p pump bottle from Muji which I took to the Ivy Club and filled up. It seemed stupid not to – it's like when you go to a hotel and take all the complimentary shampoos and conditioners – it's not because you need it. I certainly don't because I don't have any hair.

Well, I say I don't have any hair. I do – I just have a penalty spot on the back that is thinning. But I can say, hand on heart, it doesn't bother me in the slightest. I know some men freak out about losing their hair but for some reason, for someone who is ... I wouldn't say vain, I would just say conscious of his looks, it's the one thing that doesn't bother me. I'm more concerned about my eyelids drooping. It runs in the family – hooded lids, they're called. My mum had them done about 20 years ago and my two older sisters have just had them done. It wasn't a two-for-one deal, but they got a 25 per cent discount for going together. That's the only cosmetic surgery I would have, my lids – the windows to the soul have got to stay open. Imagine having your blinds half-way down all the time and not letting the light in. It's bound to depress you, isn't it?

I wonder if you could get them done on the NHS? Because you can get those lamps, can't you, when you have SAD (Seasonal Affective Disorder). It's the same thing, isn't it? Hooded lids could give you Seasonal Affective Disorder all year round.

Louie Spence

TALKING ABOUT SAD, I was feeling a little sad myself. I thought I had found the right one with Straddle-him, but not a phone call, not an email. Two weeks had gone by with not a word from Straddle-him. Was I right from the beginning, was he just another TVW? Well, we can all make mistakes.

I wasn't going to let this spoil my holiday to Benidorm with Angel Eyes. We went there every year to spend time with his family and always had a great time. The weather is always good and Angel Eyes told me that's because of a microclimate caused by the surrounding mountains. The best part is that it is close to the UK – as you all know, I hate flying.

The sea and beaches are always clean and if you want to slip away from the crowds, there are lots of hidden beaches which you can find if you know where to look. I first tried nude bathing on one of these beaches – I had never really felt confident enough before to whip off my Speedos.

It felt quite liberating, until I got out of the sea. There must have been a cold current, as I didn't feel quite so liberated when I got out, if you know what I mean. While I was on holiday I received a text from Jonathan, telling me that things were still going ahead. He was in talks with several channels and he really thought the show could be commissioned.

It was good to hear from him, but I did not want it to spoil my holiday, so I replied and asked him to email me, not text me if there was any more information. I couldn't pick up emails on my phone, so I could check on my own time. I didn't want Angel Eyes to get pissed off with me because I was working during our holiday. His time with his family was very precious to him and he did not want me to be preoccupied with other things.

It was only right really, and I did not bother to check my emails until we returned home. There was no news from Jonathan when I checked, but after about a week I got another call from him. He said he would like to meet up with me to discuss a few ideas. I told him I didn't really see the point of discussing anything if the show had not been commissioned. I could not be bothered to go out after work; even though he was quite cute, I was much happier on my sofa at home.

He was quite insistent so I decided I would meet up with him and see what he had to say. Laura and I went to meet him at a bar around the corner from Pineapple, and Laura and I looked at each other when he came in. We had forgotten how cute he was. He bought us some drinks – I had a rosé, and I ordered some chips as well. He said he was excited at the possibility of the show going ahead, and Sky1 were very interested. He thought he could be very close to sealing the deal.

AT THAT point I had a moment of panic wondering what kind of show he was going to do. Even though I had a good feeling about him, it worried me slightly that the show might go ahead. We had builders in the studios, preparations for our 30th anniversary, not to mention our members and clients – I had not really considered how they would feel about an observational documentary being filmed at the studios. I just thought it would be fun for us and we could have a laugh. I think I worried Jonathan a bit then – he had obviously been working very hard on this – when I started to raise my concerns.

He started to panic and misinterpreted my reaction as lack of interest in the project. We had a lot of high-profile clients at the studios and I knew they would not want to be confronted with a camera at nine o'clock in the morning, and there were some of our members who might not want to be filmed.

Jonathan explained that it was not really about these people – he wanted the show to be more about the people he had met when he first came in, such as me, Laura and Andrew. At this point I thought he was just trying to butter me up and it didn't work. I asked him if he thought he could make a whole show about us. I know we have a laugh and the place is different to the normal working environment, but really, a whole show? He replied that he actually wanted to make six shows (it eventually ran to 12 shows).

I thought that seemed impossible and he was just being stupid if he believed he could really base a show around a small number of people. I definitely wasn't sold on the idea. I started to lay the law down with him and that if it went ahead, they couldn't just walk around the building filming everywhere and everyone.

He reassured me that wouldn't happen and of course I did not believe him. I also told him that if the show were to be commissioned, I would want to approve the staff. If there were going to be people hanging around every day, they had to be easy on the eye, and he agreed to this. That was when I was sure he was a bleeding idiot – of course the show wouldn't happen.

So you can imagine my shock and horror when, a week later, he arrived in the studios like a cat who had got the cream. He told me that the show had been commissioned by

Sky1. I was even more shocked when he told me they would like to start filming in a month's time and they would need between three or four months to film the six episodes. My first thought was, 'I don't have the wardrobe for that length of time!'

I was quick to remind him we would get to choose the staff who would be filming us over those months. He laughed nervously and seemed to think I was joking, even though he had agreed to it before. But I wasn't joking, I was very serious.

OVER THE next week we got him to send over photographs of prospective cameramen and there may have been a thought somewhere that we could also find a husband for Laura. What a perfect way to start a love affair, with someone who would have to be around for three or four months.

Debbie Moore had met separately with Jonathan to discuss grown-up things and agreed that we would go ahead with filming the show.

We settled on one cameraman that would be based at the studios permanently, and surprise, surprise, it was our dead ringer for Johnny Depp, but more handsome in my opinion. It seemed that while he was around, no-one minded being filmed. I must admit we found it weird at first, having someone there constantly with a camera filming our mundane tasks, from taking two pounds for membership at reception to tidying the reception area, or breaking out into a song and dance on reception. There were semi-naked dancers walking around the building and they were filmed, along with the cleaning of human poo off the fire escapes, chatting to the Sugababes, Emma Bunton and Kylie. I suppose it isn't so mundane for someone who works in an office, but that was just our life.

After a week or so of having Josh around, we stopped noticing all six foot four of him. Surprisingly, most of our private-hire clients were fine with having the cameras around, as were most of our members.

I had made it clear to Straddle-him that I would want to see him every day with an update on what was going on with the show. I wanted to know what he had been filming outside of the studios, as I felt it was my responsibility to make sure that the name and reputation of the studios was treated with respect.

I had no control over individuals – the people who came to the studios could conduct themselves however they wanted. It was the employees of Pineapple that I was concerned to protect. People like Andrew were not employees of Pineapple and could do what they wanted. I suppose this is where my gay–straight relationship with Jonathan started. Often he would raise an idea that he thought would be great for filming and I would give it a flat no. He would then try to schmooze and charm me, and this became quite addictive. It would not make me change my mind, but it was great for my ego to have this straight man with buns of steel stroking it for me. My ego, that is.

I made him put his balls on the line and he promised me that he would not do anything to fuck us over, and I promised him that if he did, he would have nothing left to fuck anyone over with, and I hoped he had all the children that he wanted. At the end of the day, he was the top of the tree as the executive producer and I had put all my trust in him. We had our gay–straight lovers' tiff over the phone every day.

Different directors would come in and pretend that they had not taken note of what Jonathan had said, or what he had promised me. I would often find them filming in places they were not allowed and they would pretend that they did not know. This is where our relationship had to be strong – I knew that we did not have editorial control – all I had was his word. It can be intense to spend so much time with someone. I knew Jonathan was as passionate about what was being filmed as I was passionate about Pineapple; he understood that without my co-operation and trust, he would not have a show.

THE MORE we filmed, the more excited Jonathan became. He could feel the show was special and would be a huge hit – he thought that I would become a star. This did not impress me at all, as I had a constant battle with directors about things they were filming. I was under so much pressure so his comments seemed irrelevant to me – I felt that was the TV side of him coming out. I was only thinking about the task of keeping an eye on what the crew were doing, and keeping everyone at Pineapple happy.

As the three months drew to a close I was looking forward to the end of the show. I was taking it home with me and Angel Eyes could see the pressure I was under. He was a little concerned about this and has never liked any kind of reality programme: he finds them exploitative and mean, and hates to see people being made fools of, regardless of what they are like. So, if you are wondering why I keep calling him Angel Eyes – yes, he does have a name – and although he is happy with what is happening in my life and very proud, the last thing he wants is to be part of my public life. He is a very private person and likes to keep his life private. Our private time is very precious to him, and if I mentioned his name each time I referred to him, this book could just be about him.

This was confirmed one night when we went out to a club and when we left there was a barrage of paparazzi waiting outside. You have never seen someone move so fast and when they finished snapping, he must have been about half a mile down the road. I think that's what makes us so perfect together – in this respect we really are like chalk and cheese.

So, he had his reservations about me being part of the show when he saw my concerns. He sympathised and asked me why I thought our show would be any different from the other reality shows – why did I think we would not be exploited?

There was one reason why I thought we would not be exploited, and that reason was Jonathan – I really believed in him. I sensed something was up when, in the last week of filming show number six, he invited me out for lunch. This was obviously to tell me how amazing I had been and to thank me for my cooperation – maybe even a Rolex. But no – it was good and bad news. He said that the channel was so happy with the first two complete episodes they had seen, that even before the last four were edited, they would like to commission another six.

I thought that was great, we could do that the next year – I was just relieved to get these six shows over and done with. But he said they wanted to do the extra six shows straightaway, with no break. I nearly choked on my decaf latte. I didn't believe him and thought he was taking the piss. He knew how stressed I had been – I had to do my job while keeping an eye on the crew.

I know you are wondering, 'What job? All you did was spin around and do high kicks.' Well, yes, that was part of my job. I could not say yes to the extra six shows straight-away – I would have to go back and discuss this with every-one at work. To my surprise, everyone agreed straightaway. When I asked if they weren't finding it stressful, they all said no, it was fun. So I had been a drama queen as usual, worry-ing for everyone else when they were enjoying themselves. So, six more shows it was, and I felt much better going into these six shows knowing everyone was happy. It was just me creating drama as usual – but I wouldn't be me if that wasn't the case.

The show was close to its airing date and we were invited to a screening of the first two episodes. None of us had seen anything, so there was a sense of excitement and apprehen-sion. Jonathan had arranged for the episodes to be screened in a small cinema in Soho, for staff and crew only. There was cheap wine and nibbles, and it was very nice to be together with everyone involved. There was an excited buzz in the cinema as we sat down to watch the first show.

The opening titles came up on the screen, with 'Boogie Wonderland', and we were already laughing. I was sitting next to Jonathan with my hand in strategic grabbing distance, just by his upper thigh. But after watching the first episode I felt relieved and happy that the show was exactly what Jonathan had promised it would be. Luckily for him, I did not even have to give him a squeeze that evening.

I don't think you can ever have too much cleavage
showing, do you?

Epilogue

After the show had been on air for two weeks, I was invited on to *Harry Hill's TV Burp* to recreate my trip to Harley Street. If you have not seen the show, I went to Harley Street with my mum and my Auntie Maxine for a bit of Botox. They wanted them both on the *Harry Hill's TV Burp*, but they were on holiday at the time and I had to do it solo.

Next, all the magazines wanted to do interviews and photoshoots with me. I found it very funny that these people would be interested in just me being me. But almost 41 years old, after already living such a wonderful and full life, doing so many things I love, I never wanted to be famous. It was never one of my dreams – I felt privileged to be able to do what I wanted to do. My dreams had already been fulfilled and everything that happened after the show aired was a huge surprise to me.

I suppose the great thing is that with all my life experiences, I know to take it all with a pinch of salt. Even though

La Familia Spence.

it's a lot of fun and has given me lots of opportunities, there is nothing more important to me than my husband and my wonderful family.

If it wasn't for my mum and dad, who let me be who I was, I might not have been so confident about myself. I was able to follow my dreams of being a dancer because they let me make my own discoveries without any interference. They didn't worry about what other people might think of their not-so-run-of-the-mill son, and for that, I will be forever grateful to them.

At the moment, though, it seems there is nothing more important to them than how many times I am in the papers. I'm only joking – it gives me pleasure to see how much joy they get out of it. I mean, I never thought I would be on the *Jonathan Ross Show* with Gwyneth Paltrow, Demi Moore and Robert Downey Jr. Well, I wasn't: they were meant to be on the same day, but it was the time of the ash cloud so they were still in Hollywood. I got to share the show with Jeremy Clarkson and Paul Weller – not exactly Hollywood, but not bad after only four weeks of being on TV.

I would say that was my biggest booking up to then, but not for Pat, my mum. She was beside herself when she saw me in the *Sun*. She took it to show all the old ladies at the old people's home when she should have been feeding them. All those childhood worries when I was 12, of shaming my dad in front of his mates with my queeny ways, were a waste of time. He could not be more proud and they seem to enjoy watching me, too.

My sisters Rennie and Tania are the funniest: when they are doing their shopping in Braintree, people come up to them and say, 'Ooh, ain't your brother done well. Ain't he funny! I always knew he would make it.' They said it was funny at first, but the next person who asks will find out that in fact, no, they don't have a brother.

My little nephew, named after me, keeps telling his school teacher that his Uncle Louie wears a skirt and that it's OK for boys to wear a skirt. She didn't take much notice until he took in a picture of the two of us together, then it all became clear to her. He was not just a child with an over-vivid imagination, just one with a rather flamboyant uncle.

The question I am asked the most now is how much my life must have changed. Well, my answer to that is, yes, my life *has* changed. When I walk down the street, lots of people recognise me and want to stop and chat, which is fine if I've got the time and not rushing home to bake a quiche.

But apart from those things, and the magazines and TV, I do not feel as if I have changed personally. I can put that down to a few things. One, because of my age; two, I have true friends that no amount of money or fame could buy.

The constant love of my husband and family is the thing I cherish the most.

And to everyone reading this book, and the scaffolders, firemen, policemen, grannies and babies, girls and gays, I think it really shows what a great nation we are that I have received such love and friendship from you everywhere I go. It makes me feel very proud to be part of a society that can be so positive about accepting people for who they are, and who they are not afraid to be.

Long Live The Queen.